7600

MW00778244

To

Larine

Love and Light

Sr. Carlyne

Lost Empire of the Gods

Books by the Author

Remembering—The Autobiography of a Mystic
Secrets from Mount Shasta
The Book of Beginning Again
Revelations of Things to Come
Beyond Tomorrow—a Book of Prophecies
Shining Moments of a Mystic
Initiation in the Great Pyramid
Forever Young
The YOU Book—A Treasury of Health and Healing
The Lost Secrets of the Mystery Schools
Secret Wisdom of the Great Initiates
The Madonna and the Coming Light
Lost Empire of the Gods

****

Published by Samuel Weiser, Inc.

The Mystery of Death and Dying—
Initiation at the Moment of Death
The Eyes Have It

****

Astara's Book of Life
A series of esoteric teachings of the
Mystery Schools of all ages

****

Books in Collaboration

Kundalini and the Third Eye
with William Messick
The Mystical Marriage of Science and Spirit
by Frances Paelian
(Based on the teachings of Earlyne Chaney)
Light and Life Cookbook
with Jan and Alan Pearson

Earlyne Chaney

Lost Empire of the Gods

Astara's Library of Mystical Classics

Published by

Astara

800 W. Arrow Highway
Upland, CA 91786

Book Design: Phyllis Harrison
Cover Design: Grace Cooper

© 1994 by Astara, Inc.
All Rights Reserved

ISBN 0-918936-29-2

Library of Congress Catalogue Card: 93-72762

Printed in the United States of America

Dedication

This book was written in loving memory and recognition of the Great Ones who built the magnificent structures of Peru—

—in deep appreciation to my unseen Master teacher Kuthumi who overshadowed and inspired these writings—

—and to the Order of Melchizedek and the divine hierarchy of beings who now lead the human race toward a new earth—

and

to the few light seekers who struggled with me to the summit of Machu Picchu to bury the magnetized crystal which links this ancient mystical city with all the other Mystery Schools throughout the world where we have buried crystals in an attempt to re-establish a grid and network of light energy covering the planet—

and

especially to Edith Robbins who has traveled with me to mystical sites throughout the world as an excellent photographer without whose incredible photographs my writings and publications could never have been so vividly portrayed.

Acknowledgments

I acknowledge with profound gratitude the dedication, persistent efforts and support of my editorial assistants, Fran Blaye and Phyllis Harrison. Their attention to detail, perseverance, and relentless research in the long hours that went into the preparation of this book have been invaluable; to Edith Robbins, whose photography enhanced the experiences on the journey; and to all the other light seekers who accompanied me and made the experience a journey into light.

Contents

Machu Picchu, Lost City of the Incas

"Machu Picchu is still a lost city..."

I was standing at the summit of Machu Picchu, gazing down upon the vast incredible ruins.

"Nor is it the Lost City of the Incas..."

I was talking to myself, voicing aloud my thoughts, as I surveyed from a high point among the clouds the remnants of a city called the Lost City of the Incas. I was thinking that Machu Picchu was still a "lost" city. It takes more than massive ruins and deserted hanging gardens to make a city. It's people that make a city. And the people who built Machu Picchu are indeed "lost." Its Builders long since have vanished from planet Earth. No one knows from whence they came, where they have gone nor who they were. No one knows their purpose for building the city.

A city of the Incas? No...

If the city had been built by the Incas centuries ago, how did it come to be lost from the Incas for over 400 years? Surely, if the ancestors of the Incas built the city, there should have been some—even the peasantry—who were aware of the presence of the city. But the Incas themselves were not aware of the city until they were pressed in their flight to escape the soldiers of the invading Spanish led by Francisco Pizarro in 1532. During their 40 year battle with the relentless conquistadors, they pushed ever upward into the savage and merciless Urubamba canyon and the wilds of the Vilcapampa until in their flight they came upon—surprise!—the deserted lost city nestled on top of the mountain of Machu Picchu. They called it Vilcapampa. But their discovery of it does not mean that the Incas built the city. I believe it had to have been built by a pre-Incan civilization.

The Indians of present day Peru call the pre-Columbian people the Andenes, and credit the ancients with building and inhabiting their mighty cities and temples. All these incredible cities, temples and hanging gardens now lie in majestic ruins. The Andenes are the people that gave the Andes their name. The terraced inclines on which Peruvians grow their food crops are now called the *andenes*, because the Andenes were the strange mysterious people who taught them this method of agriculture, who carved the tiers and terraces throughout Peru, who planted strange seeds to grow their crops—so long ago that time has forgotten.

They speak of legends describing shining space-ships which brought their ancestors—the Sky People—from some distant planet. They tell of all the wondrous agricultural plants the Andenes brought, plants that were first found in Peru and carried from that land into other countries, such as the potato and corn. These were all accomplished by the people called the mysterious Andenes. And no one knows their source. Although no one knows whence they came nor where they went, no one questions that they taught the Inca race their knowledge of agriculture, of speech, of writing, of everything that leads toward civilization.

Although Machu Picchu is called the "Lost City of the Incas," no one really knows what the real name of the city was or is. It was later called Vilcapampa by the Indians because they felt the city to be sacred, and because it was on the slopes of Machu Picchu mountain where the sacred vilca plant grew—the plant that provided vilca juice which the priests drank when preparing for their initiation ceremonies. No one knows who inhabited the city, nor for how long. All that is known is that it was later taken over by the Incas and used as a secret and sacred retreat. Their holy women—the Virgins of the Sun they called them—fled there after the arrival of the Spaniards.

It is certainly believed and seemingly a fact, that even the Incas themselves were not aware of this city until the arrival of the Spaniards. When the Indians were primitive tribes it was built and in- habited by the godpeople who built it, without the Indians themselves knowing of its presence. Then, for some unknown reason, the Builders departed the city and totally deserted it for untold centuries, for untold reasons, and for untold destinations. The Indians themselves were not capable of ascending the dizzying heights, executing the journey which led up insurmountable paths, or crossing over the raging torrents of the Urubamba River. The city was there, totally unknown before the Incas found a way to span the river with rope bridges and dig a pathway to the top as a means of escaping the Spaniards. The higher they fled, the closer they came to the deserted city until, finally, they discovered it. And it was only then that they took the holy women on this very precarious journey to spend the rest of their lives in the sacred city they called Vilcapampa.

When a traveler plans a journey to Peru, uppermost in one's consciousness is Machu Picchu, Lost City of the Incas. Secondary is Cuzco, ancient capital of the empire of the Incas, which is now a bustling modern city. And Sacsahuaman, massive fortress just outside Cuzco, sheltering in its heart the lost Temple of the Sun, the Coricancha, which housed the golden *Punchao* through which the Inca priests communicated with deceased Inca kings and with, I believe, spaceships housing their extraterrestrial guardians. Other sites of mysterious temples and palaces may be sought, but few are visited because they are only now emerging from the clutches of the devouring jungles.

The visitor is apt to focus attention principally upon the massive stupendous ruins now called Machu Picchu, never once considering the contributions ancient Peruvians have made to our civilization. Usually one is not even aware that the white potato, several varieties of Indian corn and such unique drugs as quinine and cocaine came from these ancients.

Only when viewing the ruins of Machu Picchu, Cuzco and Sacsahuaman does one become aware of the remarkable technology, the incomparable genius, artistic skill, and a knowledge of bridge building and agriculture unsurpassed anywhere on our planet.

Most historians declare that all this was accomplished with no written language, not even hieroglyphics, as the Egyptians had. But that may not be true. The ancients who built the cities did indeed have hieroglyphic writing. Ruins at Tiahuanaco near Lake Titicaca in the high Andes are covered with ancient writing.

Long after their forced retreat from the Spaniards the Incas had two capitals. One was *Vitcos*, a mountain fort, which acted as a military headquarters. They later made this available to Spanish emissaries and missionaries. But Vilcapampa, their magnificent sacred sanctuary where the Virgins of the Sun had been taken, was never even whispered about in the presence of the Spaniards. Not one ever penetrated its one gateway.

Four hundred years ago, during the last days of the Spanish conquest, the last of the Incas withdrew into inaccessible parts of the Andes. Much of Peru was under control of Pizarro and his conquistadors, but these retreating Incas were shielded from their violence due to inaccessible precipices, immeasurably deep granite canyons, terrifying mountain passes, tropical jungles, dangerous rapids and equally dangerous glaciers which acted as natural shields.

When the last Inca (Tupac Amaru) departed in 1571—beheaded by the Spaniards—Vitcos was abandoned. Since it served principally as a fortress, it was found to be inconvenient as a dwelling place. Vilca-pampa, the shrine hidden among the great precipices, perched like an eagle's nest atop the peak called Machu Picchu, was completely lost. One by one the Virgins of the Sun died until the city was once more deserted. It remained so until 1911, when Hiram Bingham again discovered it. Those who had known the secret of its existence never spoke of it. Even its name was forgotten—so that when this sacred site was rediscovered four hundred years later, Hiram Bingham called it Machu Picchu (Old Peak) simply because it nestled within the embrace of the Machu Picchu mountain—and the name endured.

Chapter One

Brazil -- First Step of an Incredible Journey

The Call of Faraway Places

"Now I know..."

The words were spoken in my mind, they didn't actually pass my lips. I was gazing down in awesome wonder at the incredible beauty of Botatoga Bay as we approached Rio. There was Christ standing in majestic glory dominating the Mount of Corcovado, as if to pour down eternal blessings on a sun-drenched land. We were arriving in Rio for the first step on our journey to Brazil and Peru.

"Now I know why so many point their footsteps toward Rio de Janeiro when they think of joy, of happy vacations, of memorable honeymoons."

Who could help but think of such a city when viewing Botatoga. My heart was still radiating love and light as we landed, remembering the grandeur that was Jesus atop Mt. Corcovado. But the rays of my heart were quickly eclipsed with the first words of our guide.

"Greetings," he said, smiling with flashing white
teeth. "Welcome to Rio. But..." he stopped smiling, "I
must issue a warning to both men and women. Be
sure your wallets are securely inside your clothing.
Ladies, be sure to keep a firm grip on your handbags.
Wrap your shoulder straps firmly about your neck.
Our streets are swarming with thieving children who
are adept at snatching and fleeing with such treasures.

"And never, never leave luggage unattended in an
airport waiting room or hotel lobby. Keep it near your
feet at all times. Try to sit together as a group and keep
the luggage near your feet. Be aware at all times of the
possibility of loss.

"Try not to leave your hotel alone for sightseeing or
shopping. Have at least one partner with you. Better
still, plan such outings as a group and, preferably,
when I am along as your guide."

My heart sank in dismay. Suddenly the joy was
gone. A shadow crossed over the sun. My shoulders
slumped in sadness. Instinctively my eyes sought the
statue of Jesus, now standing lonely and forlorn
overshadowing the city, his arms outstretched in
pleaful supplication no longer heard by the populace.
My heart cried as I gazed at him, as his heart must
have cried for many years. I remembered the journey
he took to sit alone on another mountaintop long ago.

"*Jerusalem, Jerusalem, thou that killeth the proph-
ets and stonest them which are sent unto thee,*" he had
whispered, "*how often would I have gathered thy
children together, even as a hen gathereth her chicks
under her wings, but ye would not have it so!*"

Madelyn

LUXURYSUITES
INTERNATIONAL

Jesus—above Rio
de Janeiro

Is there a city anywhere on our small planet that this cosmic teacher and prophet, unseen and unheard, has not wept over? How long, Oh Lord, how long!

Realizing he had cast a pall of gloom in the stunned silence following his necessary warning, our guide turned our thoughts once more toward sights we had beheld as we flew into Rio. Not only did Christ stand dominating the city, but there in the bay rested a mammoth stone called the Petro de Gavea, the Gavea Stone. Bill Cox, traveling as leader of our tour, had already told me much about this quaint mysterious stone. He said:

"The Gavea Stone has a long history of enigma and intrigue. It is called the Sphinx of South America because it is formed in the shape of the Egyptian

Sphinx. There actually appears to be a face carved in the front of it, and many petroglyphs and inscriptions are carved on the sheer sides of the figure. Visitors to the crown of this mountain above Rio have, from time to time, seen and heard strange sights and sounds. A few have claimed physical entry through one of the three known portals. Others who say they have astral traveled into the Gavea's inner sanctum find their experiences parallel.

"They generally agree that the giant Stone is hollow. A large main chamber exists in the center of the great Stone. They say that two solid gold coffins

Gavea Stone
The Sphinx of Brazil—whose secret portals are claimed by some to be the entrance to tunnels leading throughout Brazil, just as Egypt's Sphinx is said to conceal secret tunnels.

contain dazzling, white wrapped mummies. They refer to them as the two brothers: the sacred twins, resting there in a deep sleep, perhaps awaiting some significant event. Phoenician inscriptions adorn the main chamber. A Brazilian archeologist, Bernardo Guimarais, declared he had deciphered part of the Phoenician inscriptions with: *Here rests Badezir, son of Vet-Ball of Tiru-Fenice.*

"In the smaller and adjoining room a very large goblet can be seen: it is believed to be the origin of the booming sounds emitting from the interior—like the throbbing thumps of a heartbeat. Historian Rocha Pita, author of a book on Brazilian folklore, claimed he spent some nights above the Gavea Stone and heard the low resonant thump of heartbeats issuing from the seemingly restless sphinx.

"Occasionally, when least expected, one of the Stone's three portals mysteriously opens, 'they' say, an aperture triggered perhaps by an astrological or cosmological event upon a signal from some intelligence controlling the Stone. Legend states that there are three stone doorways or portals which, under the influence of cosmic alignments, open easily. All efforts to open one of the three sealed doorways at other times have inevitably ended in failure. All manner of techniques have been employed to pry or blast open the *Lapa Portal* at the rear of the sphinx-tomb: stone wedged barriers will not budge one fraction. Yet witnesses have reported seeing the Lapa Portal—the most easily seen and accessible passageway of the three entrances—standing wide open. After running down the mountainside to relate what they saw—and returning with authorities—they found to their dismay that the entrance casements were again sealed as before.

"Unconfirmed stories state that some have never returned to the outside world once they entered the Gavea Stone. Who knows what horrors or delights await the unwary explorer? But two hikers camping near the Lapa Portal found it opened one night and supposedly ventured far enough inside to see the large chamber. They emerged. They too ran down the mountain to share their find—which again couldn't be proven by the sealed portal upon return. Brazilian archeologist, Durival Barrios, believes the Lapa Portal will never be opened by conventional means.

"These portals, especially Lapa Portal, are said to conceal entrances into inner earth and to the vast system of tunnels that are known to exist throughout South America, especially in Peru. Many feel the Gavea to be one of the entrances to these tunnels. And the Stone may be one of the ancient Halls of Records found in various sites around the planet, each of which contains records of our ancient past—our creation, our evolution, and our future.

"Brazilians have frequently reported seeing strange lights and other possible UFO phenomena above the Gavea Stone. Some believe the sphinx-tomb is a cosmic energy accumulator and generator. Magnetic radiations from the Stone—as with the Great Pyramid of Giza—seem to disrupt the sensitive instruments in nearby airplanes. It is said that the Brazilian Air Force restricts pilots from flying over the Gavea Stone."

One of the crystal shops of Ouro Preto.

The Crystals of Brazil

Our first stop out of Rio, as we were beginning our journey through Brazil, was a beautiful small town called Ouro Preto. This site is important because it is now a famous center from which one may purchase all manner of crystals. Once Ouro Preto was the richest mining town in Brazil, and a renowned intellectual center. It has now become a national monument—the entire city. All along the narrow streets of the small town there are shops, shops, shops containing all sizes of crystals and magnificent jewelry adorned with crystals. Ouro Preto translates to mean "Black Gold," but there is very little gold to be found there—black or any other color. Crystals dominate the city and we were told that the site rests upon underground caverns of crystal. They seem to be endless, apparently stretching for miles beneath this lovely little city.

Psychic Surgery in Brazil

Having been to the Philippines several times to witness and even take part in psychic surgery I was looking forward to contacting a psychic surgeon for which Brazil is famous. We found one in Dr. John (Joâo) Texeira, in his clinic at Abadiana, Goias. His spirit guide is Ignatius Loyola, the founder of the Jesuits.

It is Loyola who performs the surgery—Texeira is in a deep trance. The patients—often as many as 300 a day—are never anesthetized. Yet when any of the strange instruments used for the surgery are applied to wounds, no pain is felt. There is no laboratory, no x-rays. Loyola, working through Texeira, "sees" the problem and uses a mixed array

of instruments to operate, often a steak knife or scissors, often just his hands, passing over the affected area, to open and close the incision. There is very little bleeding involved, if any. He passes rapidly from one patient to the next.

John has been healing since the age of 12. It was then that a beau-

Dr. John Texeira.

tiful lady appeared to him and called him to his mission. He never charges for his healing. His income comes from a 2,500 acre cattle ranch and emerald mine. As our group stood inside his clinic among hundreds of others his assistant selected two of our group to assist with the healings, another lady and myself. We were to help balance and maintain all the energy flowing through him and hold instruments for him.

At one point Loyola, working through João Texeira, asked me and a medical doctor from America who was touring with us to come into a small room where he performed much of the surgery. He wanted an American doctor to witness what he intended to do. He knew I hoped for better vision in my left eye. He asked me to sit in a chair while he looked deep into the eye. Then suddenly he plunged a sharp instrument deep

With Dr. John Texeira, famous psychic surgeon.

into it. I heard the American doctor gasp, but I felt no
pain or even discomfort. Having taken part in many
psychic surgeries in the Philippines, and knowing the
patients experienced not one iota of pain and many
incredible healings, I had full faith in this young, hard-
working healer.

I saw many pictures of Jesus and Mary hanging
throughout his clinic. I saw the numerous rosaries
draping their images. I heard him pray openly for their
aid in accomplishing his miracles. So I submitted to
his drastic action with gratitude that he had chosen
me out of all our group to experience his skill as a
psychic surgeon. I feel sure the "beautiful lady" who
had appeared to him was the Virgin. And after seeing
her picture there draped with a magnificent rosary, I
submitted to his incredible surgery without flinching.
My faith in her and in Loyola was equal to that of this
unique young healer.

Afterward there was nothing obvious to show that
it had ever happened. There was no wound, and as far
as I know, no bleeding. But since I was in an altered
state of consciousness, I really couldn't be certain.
There was improvement in my sight for several years
but eventually an implant was necessary to perfect my
vision.

Chapter Two

The Nazca Lines

Entering Ancient Peru

After leaving Brazil, our first stop in Peru was in Nazca where we hoped to view the famous Nazca lines. The ancient city of Nazca lies not far from the sea in an area called the Palba valley. Both the city and the valley would long since have been deserted and forgotten were it not for the Plain of Nazca. It is in no way remarkable when one treads the earth of the parched desert. To observe its extraordinary uniqueness, one must view it from above. Only from the air can the seeker view the remarkable gigantic lines laid out in plans that could not possibly serve any purpose except as airstrips, codes or symbols. The Nazca Plain extends for 37 miles but is only one mile wide.

Archeologists seriously speak of these lines as Inca roads. But any child could quickly observe that the strips extend only a certain distance then end abruptly. Why build roads that end abruptly in the sands of the desert? And why build roads that run parallel one to the other—leading nowhere? Only airstrips are laid out according to such plans. Archeologists reject the notion of airstrips because they declare that the pre-Incas and the Incas themselves did not possess the flying ships to use them, nor did they possess equipment for surveying and creating airstrips. But since the lines could only have been mapped from the air, someone *must* have had flying ships.

One theory is that the straight lines of the Nazca plain were "route maps" for ancient pilots. Also, a piece of wood found embedded in one of the lines was carbon dated to approximately 500 B.C. Then a scientist had a hunch and stood on one of the lines at sunset on June 22. It was discovered he was standing on the line that marked sunset on the winter solstice. Further checking revealed that, assuming they had been built around 500 B.C., many of the lines marked the paths of stars and planets. Would not such a navigational chart be more needed by a pilot from another planet than one who was familiar with the local constellations?

So rarely is there any wind or rain on this high plain that there is little erosion. While walking across the lines you find that they vary from a foot or so to five feet wide, a few inches deep and are white and pebbly at the bottom. However, straight or curved, these lines make no sense at all from the ground. In fact, the Peruvian army created a 24 foot wide highway across many of the lines.

They have been preserved, measured and studied from the ground by a woman named Maria Reiche since 1946. So enthralled was this unique lady when she first saw the lines, she moved into the area, built the only "oasis" of a motel, restaurant and resting center for tourists, and spent many years of her life there. We met her during our stay when she lectured for us. She said: "The designers, who could only have recognized the perfection of their own creations from the air, must have previously planned and drawn them on a smaller scale. How they were then able to put each line in its right place and alignment over large distances is a puzzle that will take us many years to solve."

The various figures of Nazca—the spider, the hummingbird, the parrot, the man, the hands with five fingers on one hand and four on the other, the whale, the monkey, the jaguar, the condor, and others—are more than 150 yards in diameter! And the straight lines that look so much like modern runways are roughly 4,000 feet long and 60 feet wide.

Code Messages to Arriving Space Travelers?

Did the animals symbolize parts of the machines of the spaceships or different machines? Were they code signals? Did they "light up" certain animals to give messages to ancient astronauts as we illumine airfields today? There seems to have been antennae on each creature—did it house a center to communicate with the spaceships? Or could it be that those ancient space travelers who had already landed were simply giving the pilots who followed after them a quick message about the animals and humans they could expect to see on this part of the planet?

Many visitors fly over the Bay of Pisco before viewing the Nazca Plain. There, on the red wall of cliffs

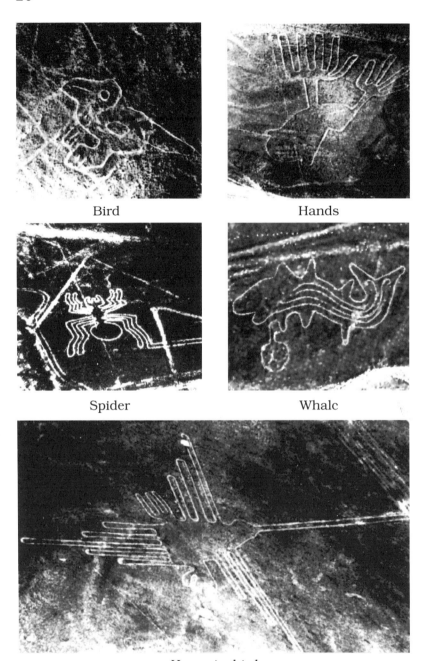

Bird   Hands

Spider   Whale

Hummingbird

surrounding the bay, one surveys a significant part of the mystery. It is the figure of a trident almost 820 feet high that can be observed up to 112 miles out to sea. What possible purpose could it have had other than to point an arriving airship in the direction of the Nazca lines? Why place it standing upright on the side of the cliff? Why make it so obvious viewed from the sea? Why so gigantic?

The long "rope" found dangling on the central column of the stone trident—what purpose did it serve? A pendulum? What could the pre-Inca people have used to create such a colossal stone signal? What machinery did they use? And why would they bother unless it was for an important purpose such as to signal approaching airships? Surely such a herculean effort had some purpose.

Why aren't our modern scientists and builders interested? Why cannot our present-day archeologists "see" the obvious purpose? Why cannot a con-

The Trident of Pisco Bay

clave of scientists and engineers meet to probe the eternal questions—rather than questioning the sanity of those who perceive the possibility of space travelers?

Those who feel that the Nazca lines may have been markers for ancient pilots have made new discoveries that seem to support their opinions. For years, there was controversy because many thought that the Nazca Plain was the only location where such lines existed. It was argued that it was some sort of religious ritual of the local tribes.

But 250 miles south of Nazca a stylized figure of a man 330 feet long, outlined with rocks, lies on top of a hill. A little farther south in Chile, another amazing find was made from the air. The plateau of El Enla-

Man

drillado is about two miles long and 870 yards wide, in the shape of an amphitheater. There is an interrupted landing strip and many symmetrically aligned stone chairs—but the beings who used those chairs must have had shins that were 13 feet long! Also found was a fallen monolith that had several faces carved on it. Now could all these figures, seen from the air, have been "signals" to arriving space travelers? Or symbols representing some code or "message?"

Also, in the deserts of Southern California—near Blythe—there is a series of large scale petroglyphs that can only be seen from the air. The style of these drawings is remarkably like those of the Nazca Plains. Could it be that these petroglyphs were "drawn" all over the world but time and weather have obliterated them in all but the driest and most remote deserts?

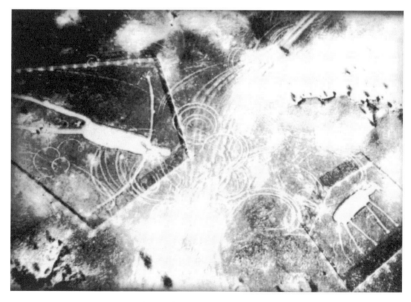

The Blythe Petroglyphs

There is much controversy over these lines but many facts cannot be disputed: because they are so large, they cannot be recognized from the ground, only from the air; they have endured for millennia; they give every indication of having been a landing field or airport for flying vehicles. The landing strips are interspersed with mysterious patterns and coded symbols of animals, birds and insects. Many of the figures of men seem to be wearing a helmet with strange rays emanating from it. A spacesuit with antennas?—telling arriving spaceships that other space travelers have landed?

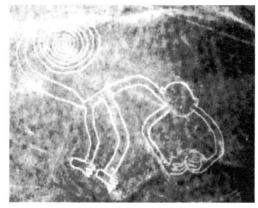

Monkey

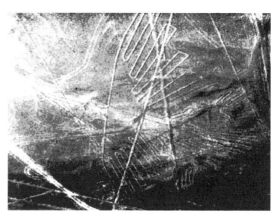

Condor

Chapter Three

The Gods of the Americas

In order to more fully understand the phenomena such as the Nazca lines, it was important for me to study the ancient myths of the Inca and Mayan world. These stories gave me a mystical perspective from which to view the temples and ruins which I visited. I'd like to share some important aspects of these ancient cultures with you now.

Viracocha—God of the Incas

As in most ancient cultures throughout the world, the Incas worshiped a number of gods and goddesses, giving them realms of power. At the top of the Peruvian pantheon is the Father God—Viracocha—the bearded White God who lives in the upper world, Juanac-pacha, with Father Sun—Inti. Mother Moon—Mama-Quilla—shares the middle world, Quai-pacha, with Mother Earth/Mother Nature—Pacha Mama. Below all these, but still a part of the Middle World, is the Morning/Evening Star (Venus)—Coleur. Then there is the Underworld, the Uku-pacha. The condor was sacred to the ancient Peruvians because they believed

25

the gods of the skies—the Sky Gods—first appeared in bird form (spaceships?). Serpents, which were called *Ama* or *Macha hui* were the symbols of wisdom; and puma a symbol of power.

Here is a poem to Viracocha which a Spanish chronicler preserved for posterity:

Viracocha, Lord of the World!
Lord of adoration.
Through art he works magic,
Even with spittle.
Who art thou?
Show thyself to thy son!
Whether he be below or above,
Or perhaps out there in the universe...

Viracocha was the "Creator of the world things." He was the teacher of his people. Like Quetzalcoatl, who appeared in Mexico-Yucatan, Viracocha came from across the sea, left via the sea and promised to return in times of trouble.

One legend about Viracocha says that he came from the sky in a golden egg and created a race of giants before he created Manco Capac, the first Inca, and Mama Occla, his queen. An incredible amphitheater in northern Chile near Tiahuanaco seems to give weight to this assertion. Scientists have said that a person sitting on one of the seats would have needed to be a giant to sit comfortably! Actually, the entire city of Tiahuanaco in the high Andes, which we shall describe later, seems to have been built by and for giants—similar to the race of Titans in ancient Greece.

Tradition declares that Viracocha was "a White God with a full beard who came over the Andean

Cordilleras from a land to the east." This "man" suddenly appeared from nowhere on an island in Lake Titicaca. The ancient Peruvians told the following story to Don Antonio de Herrera (Crown Officer of the King of the Indies and Castile), about the year A.D. 1600:

There presently appeared in the middle of the day, when the sun came out on Lake Titicaca in the Andes, a white man of a great body and venerable presence who was so powerful that he lowered the hills, increased the size of the valleys, and drew fountains from the rocks. For his great power they called him *Lord of All Created Things* and *Father of the Sun*, for he gave life to man and animals and by him notable benefits came to them. And working with these marvels he went a long way towards the north, giving on the road an order of life to the nations. Speaking with much loving benevolence, correcting them that they might be good and straight, and joining them one with another. Until the last days of the Incas, they built many temples in his name.

Quetzalcoatl—God of the Mayans

The legends and tales of three gods—Viracocha in old Peru, Bochicha in old Columbia and Quetzalcoatl in Central America—are very similar. These three reportedly came from Hy-Brazil to civilize and educate the primitive peoples of Central America and the highlands of the Andes. Hy-Brazil referred to the imperial colony of Atlantis, the home of royalty.

The traditions of Central America are replete with reports of Quetzalcoatl who taught laws, agriculture, astronomy and religion to the primitive people of those lands. The natives only knew that he came from the east—"where the sun rises and there now is nothing but water." He was the civilizer of pre-Mayan Yucatan, Mexico, and Central America.

Some say he came from Atlantis. Quetzalcoatl means "feathered Serpent." It gives one pause to remember that it was a Serpent who beguiled Eve in the Garden of Eden and persuaded her to eat the forbidden fruit of the Tree of the Knowledge of Good and Evil—so that she might become as one of the gods. Here is another great Serpent who changed the face of Central America and Mexico.

The Bible speaks of another branch of holy missionaries that perhaps arrived on the planet from another world—initiates from the Order of Melchizedek. Jesus was called "a priest after the Order of Melchizedek." These beings were called the *Nagas*, meaning the Serpents. It was these great beings to whom Jesus referred when he admonished his disciples to "Be ye wise as Serpents, but gentle as the dove."

Like the early Greeks, the pre-Inca tribes of the Andes and the Incas bestowed godhood on trees and mountains, places and people—and stones. They called the energy fused into these places and people *huaca*. Huaca was the magical power inherent in a rock, place, event, mountain, person or deity. All divine people and places possessed it. Huaca was tangible. Machu Picchu still radiates huaca. One can feel its presence exuding from every stone. Wherever huaca was felt to be strong, altars and stones, temples and plaques were built—much as the temples, cathedrals and monolithic stone sites of Europe—such as Stonehenge—were built on node points along the ley lines.

Wherever huaca was strong, or a view of one of the many distant high peaks was especially evident, the Builders had carved throne-like seats into the rock, so that one might sit and become one with the marvel of it.

We recognize their gods of the mountains as the *devas* we speak of in Ancient Wisdom. We've never doubted that each mountain, each tree, was possessed by a deva—a type of elemental god-spirit inhabiting and giving lifeforce to that site, that object, that crystal, that stone.

The Incas didn't call the mountain spirits devas. They called them *apus.* They prayed to the mountain spirit apu for its blessing and believed when icy rains fell and avalanches roared down the slopes that the apu was angry. They constantly prayed to the apu and believed that was the reason they were often blessed with unbelievable crops, incredible landscapes and sunshine. When they planted their crops on the andenes they asked for the blessings of the apu. The crops which appeared were far superior to those found in the lowlands below and in industrial and agricultural sites throughout the world. They accepted their abundance as answers to their supplications to the apu.

Because they worshipped the apus, today one often finds ceremonial sites atop many of the majestic peaks throughout the Andes. Worship in the shrines has been carried on through the centuries. Many of the smaller shrines elsewhere are piles of ritually stacked rocks called *apachita*. Ceremonial sites can also be found as one scales the trails leading to the summits, as are found on the Inca Trail leading upward from Cuzco to Machu Picchu—the remnants of the hanging gardens, the temples, the monolithic sculptures.

Even more sacred than the apu was the Earth Mother—the *Pacha-Mama*. It was she who produced the harvest together with the sunshine from the great god Inti. The apu poured down the waters for the streams, but the Pacha-Mama gave her lifeforce to fertilize the seeds of the grains, the fruits and the vegetables.

Pacha-Mama still lives—the Indians still venerate her by identifying her with the Virgin Mary—in the interior of the earth and in the most inaccessible mountainous regions. Bolivian Quechuas taught that she resided on the eternally snow-capped Mount Tunari. Many natives of the Andes still unashamedly worship the mountains and the Earth-Mother. Most of the mountains were given a gender—some male, some female. Mountaintop ritual sites were constructed, not only to pay homage to the sun and the sun gods, but to show reverence to the apu on whose peak they worshipped. Inti, the sun, with the Pacha-Mama and the apu brought about their blessings.

Though the Incas were sun-worshippers, few people realized the deep reverence they felt for the mountain peaks themselves. When the Spaniards taunted the Indians after destroying a stone idol or a captured statue, saying they had destroyed a god the Indians worshipped, the Indians viewed them with contempt. "But how can you destroy the god?" they responded. "The god we worship dwells in the mountain and in the sun."

Even today, ancient ceremonial rites are practiced among the Indians. On the surface they are good Catholics, but on certain feast days they gather together to show reverence to the sun god and the apus. To them, the Virgin Mary truly represents the divine Earth Mother—as well as the mother of the savior. Jesus, fathered by the Holy Ghost, is the son of a sun god. Apus still appear to natives during perilous journeys, sometimes in visions, sometimes in dreams. The Indians use snow and chipped ice from the mountain peaks as poultices for the ill and to cure disease, believing that these elements contain the sacred healing power of the mountain apu—the mountain deity.

Forced into Catholicism during the conquest, the majority of the Incas never truly relinquished their deep faith in their ancient gods—not only the gods of the mountains and the Earth Mother but their ancestors who came "from the sky." They never doubted for an instant that the gods from outer space had visited their land long ago and they claimed to be the offspring of these royal ancestors. The Incas sincerely believed that their ancestors had come from the sun as gods, bringing with them seeds from which their crops would grow. Many believed, too, that some animal life was also brought by the sun gods.

Pedro Pizarro said that: "A certain class among the Incas are light skinned; their noblewomen are pleasant to look at; they are beautiful and are well aware of it. The hair of both the men and the women is blond as straw, and some of them have fairer skin than the Spaniards. In this country I have seen a woman and child whose skin was unusually white. The Indians say they are the descendants of the Sky Gods. They are called the 'White Indians of Peru.' They are believed to be direct descendants of Viracocha."

The Deluge

From an Aztec Codex comes this description: "Ancient astronomers in Central and South America, peering from their high towers, noted in awe and amazement the arrival of a 'wandering planet into our earth skies.'

"There came a rain of fire. All that existed burned. Then there fell a rain of rocks and sandstone. The sky drew near the waters and the earth. The planet Venus had changed her course. There was darkness over the whole face of the earth. Men fled to caves and the rocks fell on them and shut them in forever. They climbed trees and the trees bent and shook them off. The sun went out and for five whole days no light pierced the dark blackness. Great and terrible earthquakes shook the land. Flames belched from the ground and there came a rain of flaming bodies from the heavens. Men came and went beside themselves."

From contemporary observers as far apart as Greece, Egypt, Central America, South America, Polynesia and Africa came the reports—the great catastrophe had sunk Atlantis into the depths of the ocean, followed by volcanic outbursts all over the planet. And from this destruction of Atlantis, the planet never has fully recovered.

One interpretation of the story of Atlantis given by Plato* suggests that when the armies of the Atlanteans threatened to invade Greece, Zeus and the gods of Olympus unleashed nuclear weapons against them, destroying Atlantis.

The Eternal Lamps

The mysterious central temple/cathedral of the capital of Atlantis was called Sardegon. This enigmatic temple was presumably built of white shining stones called *eternal lamps* because the light of the stones never went out. Not only the temple itself glowed with the shining light, but an altar inside held an eternal lighted lamp. The Atlanteans—and others of highly advanced civilizations—were familiar with a cold form of light that would and could not be extinguished. It did not require fuel, but burned like a natural lighted crystal. One of those eternal lamps occasionally graced the center of the gold Punchao that was reportedly placed in the middle window of the

*See *Secret Wisdom of the Great Initiates*, available from a bookstore near you or from Astara, 800 W. Arrow Hwy., Upland, CA 91786.

three windowed wall at the Torreon of Machu Picchu. I'll speak more of this later.

In the Popul Vuh (the Mayan Bible) and a very ancient Quiche Manuscript, Quetzalcoatl is said to have come from the other side of the sea, from a place called Camuhibal, described as a place of the shining white light. The ancients called it "a place of perpetual lamps."

The ancient Egyptians and Greeks were also familiar with these perpetual lamps. In the tombs of some of their immortal kings, initiates and pharaohs, it was not unknown to place an eternal lamp in the tomb, believing that the soul of the great one would be able to break the magnetic chain binding it to the mummy and unite with the spirit.

Plutarch writes of such a lamp in the temple of Jupiter Ammon. "This eternal light," says he, "could not be extinguished through wind and rain." Plutarch hinted that the alchemists created such an eternal light by reducing gold to an oily fluid. Placed in a properly constructed lamp, the gold reabsorbed its oily fluid and gave it out again. Strange objects resembling small lamps have been found in ancient graves at the ruined village of Intihuana, about 90 miles from Cuzco in Peru. These objects were composed of a material similar to glass but of an unknown chemical composition. Were these the tombs of ancients preceding the catastrophe of the Deluge?

It seems apparent that the Builders of the temple-cities of South and Central America, of Brazil and Peru vanished from the earth just prior to the great catastrophe, taking the inhabitants of special cities with them. Perhaps their insight revealed the coming of the destruction of Atlantis—whether it was by nuclear warfare or by a wandering comet.

A modern linguistic scholar has found many words that are exactly the same in Quechua—the common language of the Incas—and a Tartar-Finnish language, Chuwashen, spoken in Russia. Some words the same in pronunciation and definition are: *Viracocha*—the good spirit from space and *Kon Tiki Illa Viracocha*—ruler of the highest origin, radiant like lightning, the good spirit from space. Perhaps the space god visited the primitive people of Russia while traveling to the land of the Hyperboreans who lived at the entrance to inner earth at the North Pole.

So Quetzalcoatl, Bochicha and Viracocha, "the white, bearded men clad in robes," departed by sea to their home country or to some faraway planet from which they came. It was said that Quetzalcoatl sailed *to the east in a canoe of serpent skins.* These gods of culture, knowledge, wisdom, agriculture, religion, civilization and enlightenment took their long journey into the twilight. Not only the Incas and the Mayas, but the whole world awaits their return.

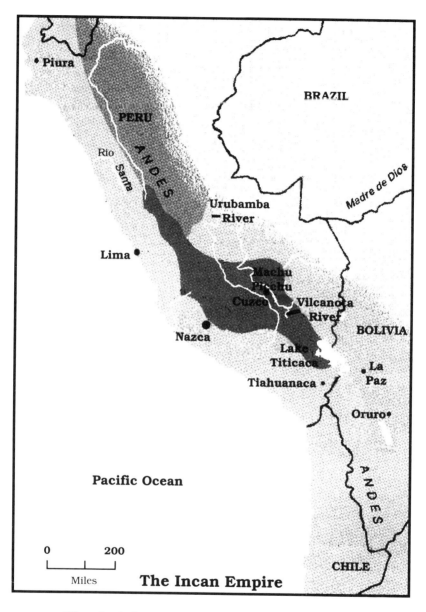

The shaded areas represent a portion of the vast
Incan Empire during the late 1400s and early 1500s.

Chapter Four

Tiahuanaco

City of the Gods

100,000 years ago...

On a 13,000-foot-high plateau straddling the border between Peru and Bolivia rests the remaining chaotic splendor of a pre-Incan civilization called Tiahuanaco (Tee-ah-wan-*ah*-co). Tiahuanaco means "City of Waning Light" in the Quechua language. But according to ancient history, Tiahuanaco was once called Chucara, which means "House of the Sun." This ancient vast ruined city lies in mute testimony of a lost glory—silent proof of the presence of great beings from another world.

When the Spaniards arrived in Peru in 1532, the Indians could tell them only that these ruins scattered throughout the high Andes were built in ancient times by a race of nameless giants. Those same giants taught them how to weave; how to build irrigation canals; and how to fertilize, plant and grow crops. They declared that this area was where potatoes were first cultivated. They said the giants who built the ancient city brought the potato and corn with them when they came to our planet from some distant star. They declared that Tiahuanaco was built by the first man who came to Earth from that distant star and it was the first city ever built on Earth.

The usual traveler reaches the towering city of Tiahuanaco from Cuzco, Peru. Sudden arrival—as by air for instance—would almost certainly leave one breathless, gasping for oxygen. Manual labor on the part of a new arrival would be totally out of the question.

How then could such an incredible city have not only been built but accommodated an obvious humanity? As one searches for telltale signs to answer the many questions, one is left groping. The city was erected on a long, narrow, horseshoe-shaped slope spread out over 24 miles. Walls are constructed of sandstone blocks weighing at least 100 tons. Topping these are smaller 60 ton blocks creating an eternal wall—eternal because the stones are clamped together with copper. Many of the enormous blocks exhibit holes at least eight feet deep.

Some believe the megalithic ruins were not originally built in the high Andes. They are believed to be a remnant of a great civilization submerged ages ago in the Pacific Ocean—ancient Mu or Lemuria. It is further believed that when the crust of the Earth upheaved during the time of the great cataclysm 12,000 years ago which destroyed Atlantis and the remains of Mu, the Andean peaks were created and the ruins of the city were elevated from the bed of the ocean.

Others declare that Tiahuanaco was a thriving city along the seashore of Peru when the great cataclysm catapulted the entire area to the Andean heights. Those who adopt this theory point to Lake Titicaca near Tiahuanaco and remind one of the chalky deposit of ancient seaweeds—a line about two yards deep. This would seem to indicate that the ridge where it is found was once an ancient seashore. Geologists state that the great upheaval—the massive universal Flood—may have raised the Pacific shore to the heights of the Andes.

No one knows for sure.

Unexplainable too are the cave paintings and pottery shards discovered on the plains near Tiahuanaco that show prehistoric (pre-ice age) animals in great detail. The fossil remains of these animals, extinct for tens of thousands of years, have been found in the same strata as Tiahuanaco. But what confuses scientists is that these remains are mixed with the remains of human occupation, when, according to their theories, humans were not supposed to be in the Americas.

Tiahuanaco-Chucara—"House of the Sun"—was both a surface city and a vast subterranean city. Many of the entrances to this "lost" city are still undiscovered. When these entrances are found, records of space travelers and their arrival on Earth may also come to light.

The monolithic statues and temples *do* suggest that the city was built by a race of giants. There is a huge paved court 80 feet square with a 45 by 22 foot covered gallery down one side—and the court and gallery are carved from one enormous block of stone. The great throne room measures 160 by 130 feet with a roof like the one in the Coricancha temple of the sun in Sacsahuaman, near Cuzco—which we shall speak of later.

One colossal statue carved in a niche of a wall is carved of human bone and depicts a man wearing a strange turban. One ear is perforated. One hand holds a scepter with the head of a condor; the other grasps a tablet with hieroglyphics. Legend states that he is called Ra-Mac, a being of a master race. His name is reminiscent of a sun god—Ra being the sun god of Egypt. Does the tablet with hieroglyphs he is holding contain a message for Eartheans, once the writings are interpreted?

Another of the ancient statues wears a beard—and the Indians of South America were beardless. Some traditions call these bearded white men the *Atumuruna*. A great quipucamayoc named Katari told Spanish chroniclers about a "very powerful lord, Huyustus," a blond, blue-eyed bearded man, king of the *Pakajes*, who ruled the Titicaca area and built Tiahuanaco over the ruins of Chucara. (A quipucamayoc was one who could "read" the knotted cords the Indians used as their form of writing and record keeping.) Huyustus corresponds to Hiracocha and may be the pre-Inca sovereign who the chronicler Fernando de Montesinos called the *Inti Capac*—the Sun-King. Two other chroniclers relate tales that it was white men who built Tiahuanaco.

Dominating the entire Tiahuanaco complex is the largest structure of the city, the Temple of Kalasasaya. Only a giant could easily execute its stairs which, carved from a single block of stone, are too wide and too high for mere mortals to climb. Its massive portal, with its equally massive stones dovetailed to perfection, opens to a courtyard strewn with fallen and upright giant-sized idols. In Incan times, the steps from the temple were in Lake Titicaca—now about 15 miles away—and the water level is still dropping. Who carved and placed the monolithic sandstone statues, some with four fingered hands? Who can read the message in their quiet piercing eyes that stare out at a vast wasteland pregnant with incomprehensible messages?

The carvings on the walls of the subterranean temple of Kalasasaya rival Earth's most stupendous

The incredible massive statuary of Tiahuanaco.

art gallery, so intricate are the faces emblazoned there, reflecting varied human physiognomies.

The masks of faces bordering the temple wall feature the faces of various races. Some appear to be Englishmen with narrow lips. Some possess long noses and some noses are hooked. Some wear turbans and twelve symbolic braids—and turbans were worn in Israel until 1000 B.C. Some are Negroid. One has Egyptian eyes and the colors of a high priest of a sun god wearing a large mitre on his head. Some say the mitre contains symmetrical symbols resembling a map of the world. Others declare the mitre contains a symbol of a sun god.

The ears on the carved heads range between petite and abnormally thick. Some, like those on Easter Island, exhibit enormous elongated earlobes. Some exhibit rounded features, some angular. The most mysterious feature of the masks is that many wear peculiar helmets. What is the mute message these lifeless faces convey? The artist who carved the faces must have been familiar with the varied races of the entire planet. And if this *was* the first city built on Earth—and it may well have been—the artist must have known the various races which would be dwelling here in cities of the future.

In the center of this Temple's courtyard stand three obelisks, one the renowned idol *Kon-Tiki*—an enormous block of red sandstone 24 feet tall and weighing at least 20 tons.

Rising above these magnificent ruins stands the enormous pyramid of Akapana. Ages of weathering

The renowned obelisk of the idol Kon-Tiki—an enormous block of red sandstone 24 feet tall and weighing at least 20 tons. He appears to be wearing a helmet of some sort. Could the symbolic carvings he holds in his hands be a coded message to Eartheans?

and vandalism have almost destroyed what was once a chapel on its summit, obviously for religious festivals or ceremonies, perhaps for initiation—as was and is the King's Chamber in the Great Pyramid. Akapana appears to be a sister of the Pyramid of the Moon we saw at Tiatihuacan near Mexico City.

Standing before this great pyramid at Tiahuanaco is a most mysterious artifact called the Gateway of the Sun, the most renowned of all the city's structures. This stupendous edifice is constructed of one single block of hard stone and weighs more than 10 tons. It is 16 1/2 feet wide and nearly 10 feet high. It is lavishly carved and the carvings could only have been achieved through the use of tools not familiar to the primitive tribes of ancient Peru. In the center of the lintel is a symbol representing a sun god—or more likely, a space traveler.

This immortal being has hands and feet and each hand grasps a scepter, perhaps representing a wand or a weapon. Legend declares this central figure is perhaps Viracocha himself—or Lord Maru, the great being he brought with him when he landed his shining spaceship at Tiahuanaco. Lord Maru was left on Earth when Viracocha departed. The figure in the center of the lintel is surrounded by 48 figures with wings. They could represent the astronauts traveling with Lord Maru.

Some of the figures in the Gate of the Sun have only four fingers—which seems to embellish the legend of another golden spaceship that arrived ages ago bearing to Earth a goddess named Orejana. She came to

The most mysterious edifice of Tiahuanaco is the Gateway of the Sun, constructed of one single block of hard stone weighing more than 10 tons, 16 1/2 feet wide and 10 feet high. The sun god—or space traveler—in its lintel (pictured below) has hands and feet and each hand grasps a scepter. He is surrounded by 48 figures with wings.

mate with Eartheans to bring forth advanced earth beings—offspring having an earth father and a space mother. The legend tells us that after giving birth to 70 earth children, she departed the planet and returned to her home among the stars. Thus she planted the seeds of an advanced civilization among the Indians. Orejana had only four fingers.

'Midst the scattered stones of the city lies an enigmatical calendar. One glance reveals that beings more highly evolved than present Eartheans created such a calendar. It speaks silently of the equinoxes, the movements of the moon, the astronomical seasons. It considers the rotation of the Earth.

It is covered with hieroglyphic symbols, a mute denial that the ancients possessed no form of writing. Some who have striven to interpret the hieroglyphic symbols state that they record the placement of the planets and the heavenly bodies 27,000 years ago. Some say 100,000 years ago. Do they also contain symbolic messages for Eartheans, identifying the Builders of this megalithic marvel?

The calendar and the message of the hieroglyphs remind me of another calendar I saw on the ceiling of a small room in the temple of Dendera in faraway Egypt. Standing enraptured at the sight of it, I suddenly remembered what the mystic Paul Brunton had written about it many years ago—that it charts the state of the heavens over Egypt at least 90,000 years ago. The original almost certainly was brought from Atlantis to Dendera in the distant mists of time.

The enigmatic calendar covered with hieroglyphic writings. Could these writings contain messages for Eartheans?— who these Builders were, where they came from, why they departed Earth?

Enormous stones dovetailed to perfection.

A stairway carved from a single block of stone, so massive only a giant could execute—too wide and too high for mortals to climb.

Immense stone columns.

Viewing such a calendar at Tiahuanaco and such a massive great idol with its enigmatic hieroglyphic symbols, created possibly 27,000 years ago, suggests to many observers the presence of extraterrestrials... the presence of those far beyond us in culture and in evolution.

When will archeologists dig deep at Tiahuanaco so we may learn what secrets are still beneath it? There are artificial mounds with perfectly level tops that cover an area of 4,784 square yards. No excavations have been performed on these obviously artificial hills. What lies beneath them?

Tiahuanaco has been systematically looted and vandalized more than any other archeological site in the Western Hemisphere. The Incas were awed by the ruins but the conquistadors quarried the pre-cut stones for their buildings there. Sculptors carved Christian statues from the pillars. A tribe of nearby Indians has been using stones from the city to build their village. But the worst vandalism of all was the massive dynamiting to build the Guaqui Railroad at the turn of the century. How many priceless artifacts were lost to the rampant destruction?

Old photos show the progressive destruction of this wonderful site. One piece called *The Friar* was relatively well-preserved until a few years ago. Now the hieroglyphs have all but been erased and part of its head has been chipped away.

Engineers and researchers are astonished by the incredible ruins of what could be an enormous drain-age system found in the outer walls of Kalasasaya

which point to an obvious knowledge of advanced
architectural structures—certainly beyond that of the
Peruvians of that distant time. The mysterious water
conduits—or conduits possibly housing an astonishing electrical system—are thrown aimlessly about the
ground as if a giant earthquake hurled them heedless-
ly and without purpose. They measure six feet long
and one and one half feet wide. These conduits
surpass our modern concrete conduits.

The conduits have a modern shape with smooth
cross sections, polished interiors and exteriors and
precise edges. Half pipes have grooves and protru-
sions that fit closely together. There are double pipes
carved out of one rock. And there are many with
absolutely precise right angles. But why have only the
top parts of many of the pipes been found?

The upper part of a water pipe is not absolutely
necessary, but the bottom is essential. Were these
actually water pipes? A being with the technology to
create such perfect work would not have created two
pipes in one conduit for water. One can double the
amount of water passing through by simply making a
single larger pipe. And right angles will merely trap
debris and water in the corners. And why are there a
large number of pipes that only display the top half of
the pipe?

Our modern knowledge makes it seem more probable that these were conduits to hold energy cables.
Lasers and complicated tools and other electronic
equipment require cables for power. Admittedly there
could have been some sort of beamed energy trans-
mission, but it would have been incredibly awkward to

aim it properly. Cables make more sense because a very controlled amount of energy could be delivered with less chance of mishap.

It seems obvious the inhabitants deserted the city suddenly. Why so abruptly? Did they know of the coming catastrophe and flee before it struck? What could have caused such an obvious upheaval of enormous blocks and statues except a wandering satellite as ancient legend suggests?—an incredibly stong earthquake—or perhaps a pole shift?

Local legends also speak of the secret entrance at Tiahuanaco to the immeasurable tunnel which leads to Shamballa, the city of inner earth or to the inner world of Agharta. This legend—if it be a legend—speaks of a civilization in inner earth, a Shangri-La with a labyrinth of tunnels and underground passages linking Shamballa and Agharta with other subterranean worlds. These inner world cities presumably were once inhabited by a race of people who escaped the tremendous cataclysms that destroyed much of the surface world. Such a legend is separate and apart from the knowledge of the long tunnels of Peru, Brazil and even Mexico. I have discovered similar endless tunnel legends in many countries around the world. Nor can they be treated with disdain since our own space planners speak openly of building bases on the moon—all underground.

The Legend of Viracocha

Inca legend says that a great sun god first arrived on Earth in long ago Peru. His name was Viracocha.

He brought with him a being named Lord Maru who was left by the unconquerable Viracocha to civilize humankind. The legend continues that Viracocha, arriving from some distant planet in a massive spaceship, brought with him an Ark of the Covenant which contained laser ray instruments with which to build the enormous structures and cities strewn throughout the jungles of Peru. The legend says the shining spaceship first landed on the Island of the Sun in the middle of Lake Titicaca, near the ruins of Tiahuanaco, 13,000 feet above sea level. The Inca Indians vow it was Maru and his godpeople who built Tiahuanaco.

We do not know a great deal about the Ark of the Covenant that the space gods brought to Peru, but there is a detailed description of how to build one in the Bible. If the directions given to Moses in the Bible were followed, a several hundred volt electrical condenser would be created. The condenser was formed by the gold plates and a positive and negative conductor. The crown and border would have charged the device. If one of the cherubim on the mercy seat was a magnet, it would act as a loudspeaker. The Bible says the Ark was often surrounded by flashing sparks and that Moses, closed away in a specially constructed tent, used it to communicate with the Lord whenever he needed help and advice.

Continuing the Andean legend, Lord Maru instructed his highest initiates to choose wives and husbands from among the primitive Peruvian people so that the offspring, born of an Earth mother and a god father—or vice-versa—could accelerate civilization on this planet. The space gods and goddesses arriving on Earth were highly advanced beings with a physical form and blood different from the races of Earth. On the immense plateau where Tiahuanaco became a civilization, the godmen and goddesses, mating with the primitive forms of Earth, created an offspring of earth-space heritage. The three tribes dwelling therein were the earth born, the earth-god born, and the white skinned gods and goddesses from faraway planets.

Archeologists and anthropologists agree that the earliest civilizations they know of around Lake Titicaca worshipped a jaguar god. The scientists were all amazed when they began seeing satellite photos and discovered that Lake Titicaca and a smaller lake nearby were shaped liked a jaguar chasing a rabbit. The rabbit is the smaller lake. This observation is only obvious from spaceflights as Lake Titicaca is 122 miles long, up to 47 miles wide and covers over 3,200 square miles. Like the Nazca lines, such a revelation could never be detected from ground observation.

There are scores of islands in Lake Titicaca—from small uninhabited rocks to huge islands with mammoth stone temples, terraces and giant ruins. The local Indians, the Aymara, say that Titicaca means "rock of the jaguar" in their language, while to the Quechuas it means "rock of lead."

Lake Titicaca, rising 13,000 feet into the crystal air of Bolivia, is definitely overshadowed by a female deity. She is also sacred, not because of the deity alone, but because it was upon the Island of the Sun in her midst that the sun gods first landed in the

Lake Titicaca

It was on the Island of the Sun in Lake Titicaca where
Viracocha first arrived in a shining spaceship, bringing
with him Lord Maru and a host of other space beings. It was
on this island, too, that the first Inca appeared—Manco
Capac—son of Viracocha or Lord Maru and an earth
mother. It was he, using an Ark of the Covenant, a laser
instrument, who built many of the massive structures of
early Peru—such as Sacsahuaman and the Temple of the
Sun—the Coricancha—inside the massive fortress. And it
was Viracocha and Lord Maru, says the Inca legend, who
built the incredible city of Tiahuanaco nearby.

shining spaceship. It was on the Island that Manco Capac, the first Inca King, was born. For centuries a festive ceremony was celebrated on the Island expressing reverence to Viracocha and the Sky Gods. The native Indians never once doubted that it was the Sky Gods sent by Viracocha who built the magnificent city of Tiahuanaco nearby.

According to legend, with the power of the Ark— laser beam instruments capable of nullifying gravity —Viracocha, Lord Maru and his companions built this incredible city. There the legend ends and reality begins. The remnants of once glorious Tiahuanaco still span the highest peak of Bolivia.

Today Tiahuanaco lies a magnificent ruin. Not even legend tells us why the city was built, who built it, whence came these mysterious Builders—nor where they went when they suddenly departed Earth. And the Island of the Sun, where Viracocha—and Orejana with the four fingers—first landed, still lies in the midst of Lake Titicaca, covered in ruined temples and palaces.

Like the culture of Egypt, Tiahuanaco seems to have sprung forward into an instant remarkable civilization. It happened suddenly, a miracle city—there seems to have been no gradual process of evolution here. Certainly Tiahuanaco does not follow the local traditions and architecture because those were primitive. Suddenly there was a stupendous city, built of enormous stones and statues and following an unknown architecture. No one tries to give an age to this city—tradition runs the gamut from 12,000 to 100,000 years old. But no one really knows when it was originated or how it came to be there, or who built it. Tiahuanaco simply IS.

The city boasted pyramidal platforms, incredible canals, great stairways and the use of massive stones as building material. From all indications, Tiahuanaco was inhabited for several centuries and then, suddenly, its inhabitants vanished from the face of the Earth.

Was Tiahuanaco the Cradle of the Human Race?

When the Indians first found Tiahuanaco in 1438 A.D., the stone city was deserted. Because of the size of the pyramids, the palaces, the monuments, they concluded the city was built by giants. The Tiahuanaco complex covers about 175 square miles. Arthur Podnansky spent most of the early 1900's studying Tiahuanaco, and he (among others) believed it was several thousand years older than the pyramids of Egypt. It may have been the cradle of the human race—which in no way cancels the notion that the city was built by gods and goddesses from another planet. Metal clamps and rivets in some of the buildings are identical to metal clamps and rivets in Assyrian palaces in Mesopotamia. The gods the researchers can identify also seem to be the same as Mesopotamian gods from the 5th to 3rd century B.C.

Hieroglyphics in Tiahuanaco—as much as can be interpreted—indicate that a lost satellite crashed to Earth and caused cataclysms which stripped the summit of Bolivia of rain forests and transformed it into a barren altiplano. They also indicate that, before the cataclysm that brought volcanic eruptions, earthquakes and floods, the inhabitants of Tiahuanaco fled in different directions, many arriving in Egypt, Tibet, China, Cambodia, Mexico. With the arrival of the Tiahuanacans in Egypt there came also a sudden miraculous advance in Egyptian civilization. Perhaps the builders of Tiahuanaco also brought to birth the high civilization of Egypt—Thebes, Memphis, Abydos, Heliopolis, Karnak and the Great Pyramid.

Space travelers presumably also arrived in Egypt in spaceships during the reign of King Zoser 5,000 years ago, bringing with them knowledge of architecture, art, and a new religion—sudden developments in Egyptian culture. The area of Sakkara in Egypt was patterned after the city of Chucara (Tiahuanaco) in the Andes, the difference being that Chucara was mostly underground while Sakkara was a surface domain.

Zoser's Step Pyramid at Sakkara was built by Imhotep, prime minister of Zoser, an admitted godman of his time. Imhotep was a philosopher, doctor, high priest of the Mysteries, scribe and architect all merged into one incredible being. Before his arrival, Egypt was still in the midst of primitive methods of civilization. Within fifty years after his arrival, Egypt leaped forward several thousand years in technology and civilization. Perhaps he was a space traveler from Chucara-Tiahuanaco. According to archeologists, the only building tools available to Imhotep were wooden wedges and copper, both unsuitable for cutting granite. But the 197 foot tall Step Pyramid was surrounded by a magnificent White Wall 33 feet tall and 1,750 feet long which was so masterfully built it was never truly equalled by later builders. So he *must* have had advanced technology and the instruments necessary to achieve his purposes.

After establishing Tiahuanaco as a sacred city, Lord Maru journeyed to the peaks of the Picchus in Peru, and there established another sacred city— Machu Picchu. There—and in Cuzco too—his initiates mated with the Indians and established another civilized center.

After witnessing these marriages and the planned acceleration of Earth's inhabitants, Lord Maru departed Earth to return home.

Even today Tiahuanaco gives evidence of a civilization advanced far beyond our own. There is little doubt for many that the god depicted in the center of the lintel on the Gate of the Sun at Tiahuanaco was the leader of the Sky People and the 48 figures surrounding him were his traveling companions—all sent by Viracocha to establish their seed on planet Earth.

The natives of Tiahuanaco still make seasonal offerings to the gods, asking for favorable weather and good crops. They ceremonially throw their offerings into Lake Titicaca. Perhaps that is why, even now, we pause to toss a coin in a fountain or a stream, making our "wish." Ancient ingrained traditions die hard— perhaps they never die.

Chapter Five

Manco Capac and the Golden Staff

The First Great Inca

Thousands of years ago the first great Inca, *Manco Capac,* came on the earth scene. His presence is not legend. It is history. The fact that he possessed qualities far beyond the usual Earthean is also history. All of the ancient manuscripts assert that he was the son of Viracocha or Lord Maru himself. We do know he had to have been sired by one of the gods because of the powers, the insight, the purity and the wisdom he exhibited. His mother was an Earthean— thus he was a demigod and was accorded the recognition of a king. From this first semi-divine Inca, the other Incas descended, each becoming less divine until they finally became quite Earthean.

According to the legends, the Island of the Sun in Lake Titicaca was the birthplace of Manco Capac and his wife-sister, Mama Occla, a demi-goddess. During a time of darkness on the island there rose a great light. The sun god brought these two beings out of the resplendent light—Manco Capac and Mama Occla.

Those who came with Lord Maru called themselves "Children of the Sun." Inca means *Lord of the Sun* and Manco Capac was the first being called Inca.

Manco and Occla were told they were to bring solace and well-being to a suffering world. They were told they must leave Tiahuanaco to bring knowledge to the peoples dwelling in the lands below—guidance in building their villages and growing crops. Lord Maru gave Manco Capac a golden staff topped with a magnificent rainbow. Departing Tiahuanaco, Manco and Mama Occla were to take the staff with them and travel throughout the lowlands seeking a site where the staff would sink easily into the earth. That was to be the site of the city Manco was to build.

After much traveling he and Mama Occla found such a site where Cuzco is now located. The staff sank suddenly and deeply into the earth. With the laser rays of the Ark of the Covenant—the golden staff and its "rainbow"—Lord Maru, Manco and his followers built the fortress of *Sacsahuaman* overlooking the city of Cuzco. The tribe of Indians inhabiting the area at that time was called the *Wallas*. Having no tools, no derricks, no pulleys, no wheels, no draft animals, no iron and no steel, the Indians could never have built such a magnificent structure as Sacsahuaman.

The principal cities of the great civilization of the Inca included Tiahuanaco high in the plateaus and canyons of Bolivia, and Machu Picchu hidden among the giant precipices of Peru. Manco Capac, dwelling first in the dizzying heights of Lake Titicaca and Tiahuanaco, and later in the sacred heights where

Cuzco lies, was worshipped as a demigod, the son of the sun—or the son of the sun god.

Sacsahuaman

Sacsahuaman—where the golden staff sank into the earth—is the largest megalithic fortress in the world. We stand in awe, even of the ruins, because it is obvious it was built by incomparable masons as well as artists of stone architecture.

This Pre-Incan fortress, built on the rocky spur of K'embo near Cuzco, was linked at one time with the mysterious stone temple of Stonehenge in England and another at Carnac in France. Was the site of Sacsahuaman selected because of electromagnetic currents surging through the earth at this location? Certainly to view this massive fortress should convince observers of the presence of titanic forces. Only titans could have brought these stones to this site. What did the Builders use to dress the stones—and were they placed in this particular spot for a certain purpose?

The megalithic stones weigh as much as 300 tons each and are as tall as 16 1/2 feet. The joints, without clamps or cement, are dovetailed so accurately even a knife blade cannot be inserted. These stones were hauled from quarries over a mile away. They've withstood earthquakes and everything else nature in the Andes could throw against them. They are carved to fit their own structured locks and keys. Some of the walls are 1500 feet long. There are three zig-zag walls that extend for about 375 yards with 21 battlements.

Sacsahuaman

It must cover a great "huaca" (energy) point, a node of the crystal grid spread over the entire planet—else why did Manco Capac's golden staff suddenly sink into the soil, marking the place where a great civilization center was to be built?

Oh, the questions! Could it be that the titans who came with Manco Capac, knowing the natural crystal grid of the earth, chose the site for Sacsahuaman and these stones because energy centers and particular radiations—their huaca—were there? Else why did the mysterious staff carried by Manco Capac suddenly "sink into the earth" at Sacsahuaman? Some cosmic current must have been responding to his staff—his rod of power. And why transport the mammoth stones so far unless a powerful huaca radiated there?

Did all these megalithic stones form part of a previous universal building complex? A lost city lies underneath the existing ruins—this is known. This is the only certainty concerning Sacsahuaman—that a great complex of some sort and for some purpose was built by a method unknown to us today—built and already destroyed *before* the present fortress of Sacsahuaman was built. So when Manco's golden staff with its magnificent "rainbow" sank into the earth at Sacsahuaman, it must have been responding to natural huaca energy nodes already discovered and enhanced by a previous group of Sky Gods.

Inside the present Sacsahuaman fortress there is another calendar—the celebrated Calendar of Sacsahuaman. What does the Calendar foretell? Or measure? Some feel that it is a graphic representation of the *ceques*—ley lines—that divided the empire of Tahuantinsuyo (now called Peru) from its center at Cuzco.

The Incas had a tradition that warriors were required to thrust their weapon hand into the head of a snake carved into one of Sacsahuaman's monolithic rocks. It was said to give them strength, courage and magical protection in battle. Today, when one thrusts a compass into that snake's head, the needle spins wildly.

More than 4,000 people were permanently employed in Sacsahuaman—priests, all types of servants, shepherds of the ecclesiastical flocks, porters, sweepers, and especially the Virgins of the Sun—the aclla. Secondary chapels were devoted to Illapa, the god of thunder and lightning, Coleur the evening star, and to the rainbow.

Spanish chroniclers saw Sacsahuaman as such a majestic work that they were quite sure magic was used in its construction. One said it was raised by the black arts; two said the devil built it. Three thought it to be the work of giants and three others believed the Incas knew how to melt rocks. Two said some ancient waters turned trees to stone and by the 1800s writers suspected that the Incas had an herb for softening and shaping rock.

Many believe—and with just cause—that the Incas knew how to harness the sun's energies to cut and fit the incredible stones. Venerating the sun as they did, they could have used reflectors to concentrate the sun's rays to carve the stones—parabolic dishes shaped like TV satellite dishes. The theory could be correct because the very shape of some of these colossal stones could not be achieved by any tools we possess even today.

Coricancha—Temple of the Sun

Inside the massive fortress of Sacsahuaman, Lord
Maru and Manco built the Temple of the Sun—the
Coricancha or *Inticancha*—renowned for its magnificence. No temple in the empire held as much prestige.
This was the center of worship for the high priests—
commoners were not allowed to enter. It was the size
of four football fields and was located in the most
historical part of the fortress. At its heart was the
sacred place where Manco's staff sank.

The roof and walls of the Coricancha were covered
with thick plates of gold. Part of this temple complex
was an *Intipampa*, a courtyard of the sun, with a small
walled "garden" in a corner of it. Inside the Coricancha
Manco Capac constructed a solid gold symbol of the
sun around the Ark that Lord Maru had given him.
This dazzling, glorious sun of purest gold with its
extending rays graced an entire wall of the Coricancha. The mammoth golden symbol was placed so that
sunrise focused its beams on its golden rays, causing
a brilliance the human eye could not behold. The rays
of the sun symbol shone like sparkling diamonds.
These golden rays were thickly encrusted with emer-
alds and other gems of unbelievable brilliance.

The beautiful golden sun symbolized the sun of our
solar system. The glorious center of effulgence usually
contained in its heart the Ark of the Covenant used for
communicating with the space gods Viracocha, Lord
Maru, and all the other godbeings who came to Peru
in its early days—the Titans who built Tiahuanaco,
Machu Picchu, Sacsahuaman and all the other mag-

nificent temples and cities now devoured by the jungles of Peru, Bolivia and Brazil. This center—called the *Punchao*—performed the same function for the Incas that the Ark of the Covenant did for Moses in his tent in the desert. That is, a communication center through which Eartheans could communicate with space commanders circling Earth in their space-ships—and also to neutralize gravity when necessary.

The Ark of the Covenant—the Punchao, an ora-cle—could be removed from the center of the sun symbol and another center substituted. Seven such centers existed. Mystics, and those familiar with the oracles of Egypt and Greece, realize that through an oracle the voices of deceased Ptahs and Melchizedeks could speak. In other words, Lord Maru also brought from his home planet a communication system called a Punchao through which the space gods and revered spirit teachers could speak to the Inca, guiding him in all matters—just as Jehovah or some other guiding force spoke to Moses. An Ark of the Covenant or any of its other seven centers could be inserted in the center of the sunburst to establish a station of com-munication wherever the Punchao was carried.

The Punchao was molded in the shape of an Inca seated on a gold *tiana* (throne). From the throne there arose, "like a sugarloaf," a golden chest containing the pulverized hearts of dead Incas. It was from this form that the voices spoke—the words of the unseen hi-erophants speaking to the priests of the temple, guiding them, prophesying to them, and sanctifying them from their unseen spaceships or from their realms in spirit land. The belief was that the apu of the

Punchao carried the Incas to heaven at the time of their deaths and carried their knowledge back to the people of Tahuantinsuyo (Peru).

Another of the removable seven centers of the sun symbol was a shining white stone. It was called *Iuracrunu* by the Incas. The enormous white stone was a brilliant crystal which also appeared to have the mystic properties of an oracle—much like the Urim and Thummim on the breastplate of the high priest of the old Jewish temples. This Jewish breastplate was patterned after the ancient Egyptian breastplate of the Goddess of Truth—Themei—who was identical with the Greek goddess Themis. During the ceremonies of initiation which occurred in the Coricancha, voices of unseen hierophants spoke through the oracle of the crystal revealing secrets to the new initiates only the sun gods could impart.

For instance, they revealed only to the initiates of Coricancha the knowledge of the chinkanas, the labyrinthine tunnels of Peru with their innumerable socabons (chambers). The labyrinth under Sacsahuaman was so complicated that even the Inca needed a guide to visit it. Entrances were only revealed to the high priests and certain initiates. The high initiates were also taught how to read the hieroglyphic writings which could be discerned on the golden symbol only when the sun rays struck it at a certain angle at a certain hour of the day.

The mystic writings revealed the secrets of the tunnels and the mystical formula which opened the entrances, some of which were found beneath the

Coricancha. One immense subterranean tunnel extended from Cuzco to Lima, a distance of 380 miles. Then it turned to enter Bolivia, extending 900 miles toward Tiahuanaco. Doorways or portals throughout the tunnels could only be opened by the hierophants and initiates who could give the secret signs and speak the secret words.

After the Spanish Conquest, the Dominican priests used the stones and the foundation of the Coricancha to build a Catholic church—after the Temple of the Sun was destroyed and all of its gold stolen. In May, 1950, an earthquake shook Cuzco and the Dominican church was leveled. After removing tons of shattered masonry and scraping away paint and plaster to begin the renovation, something wonderful was discovered. Most of the ancient structures of Coricancha were found intact, quite undamaged by the quake. Peruvians hoped to reconstruct the Coricancha, but the hope proved futile because the Catholic church was quickly rebuilt.

Chapter Six

Cuzco, the Chosen City

The Puma

Cuzco, including Sacsahuaman, is truly the archeological treasure of Peru and is built in the shape of a puma. The fortress of Sacsahuaman, just northwest of the city, is considered the head of the puma. In the museums, one finds the treasures of the history of the Incas—the sons of the Golden Sun, the Indians with their rainbow colored costumes. An early Inca named Pachacuti banished the original inhabitants to make Cuzco a religious and ceremonial center.

From the beginning of the Inca Empire, Cuzco has been called the "navel of the world"—which means it surely was a chakra, or energy center in the earth-cosmic grid. And it was a planned city from the beginning. Two rivers, the Huatanay and the Tullumayo, were channeled to flow east and west of the town. A modern Peruvian living there says he has watched laborers remove ancient solid stone bridges to build a modern avenue across the river. The main part of the city between the rivers was a little over a mile long and 450-650 yards wide and the streets were paved and had central gutters. The streets were also arranged in a slightly trapezoidal pattern, as were most of the doors and windows throughout Tahuantinsuyo. There were five fountains and an advanced irrigation system that brought fresh water to the city. There were hundreds of royal storehouses built on the hills southwest of the town proper that were separated by six to ten feet to help prevent devastating fires.

Many of the doorways were topped by monolithic lintels weighing several tons—as were those we found at Eleusis in Greece. And found again in Ephesus in Turkey when we visited those ruins seeking the legendary home of the Blessed Virgin. One ceaselessly wonders how, with no derricks, those remarkable masons ever lifted the lintel stones.

It has been surmised they raised a lintel by building a mound of earth and stones in front of the doorway—similar to the legendary ramps of Egypt— then with pulleys, maneuvered the lintel into place, after which the mound or ramp was removed. But if raising such a lintel represented such a herculean task, why not use an ordinary lintel?—Why such a mammoth stone? Was there an undiscovered purpose? Who measured the lintel stone? Who cut it to exact proportions? And how was it *really* lifted? Levitation?

It was the Incan palaces around the square which captivated the Spaniards. Bernabe Cobo noted in his Historia del Nuevo Mundo: "The walls are the only remarkable point of these edifices. But these walls are so extraordinary that it is difficult for anyone who has not contemplated them to appreciate their perfection. …One easily imagines the enormous expense of energy which the exact fitting of these blocks represented. Every surface of the block was precisely cut to correspond to the opening for which it was intended. Such a job must have required infinite patience. In order to obtain such a perfect adjustment, it was necessary to position the block, remove it, reshape it and reposition it over and over again until it fit"…

The Spanish estimated there were 10,000 homes in the Cuzco valley when they first arrived. Each home compound was constructed around a courtyard with only one entrance. Once inside the courtyard each home in the compound was a two-or three-story building housing various branches of the same family—as if each family occupied its own apartment, sharing a single courtyard and entrance. There were no locks and keys on these entrances because there were no thieves before the arrival of the Spaniards. Across the door on the inside of the opening was a bar-hold anchored in the wall.

Usually, when an Indian departed his home, the doorway was left open to indicate that the master was not at home. Often across the open doorway was simply a little bamboo stick inserted into the bar-hold. Such a stick was a sign that no one was to enter. With the arrival of the Spaniards and their methods of home building, the Indians quickly learned about locks and keys. They understood they were used to prevent thievery and for this they despised the Spaniards. In many Quechua villages, even today, a person can be forever exiled from his people for theft.

Many of the present-day inhabitants of Cuzco live in homes with at least one wall made of Incan stone. The great plaza—then called Haucaypata, now called the Plaza de Armas—is much the same as it was in the days of the Incas, and often used for the same kinds of festivals and rituals. Now, however, instead of parading the mummies of Incas around the plaza for all to see, statues of Jesus and Mary are carried by devout Quechua.

A massive gateway, Rumicolca, in the road at the southern end of the Cuzco valley, acted as a tollgate to the city, as did a similar gate to the north. Their purpose was to check everything departing the city to assure that no gold, silver, or good cloth was being taken away. Entry into the city was barred between sunset and sunrise. And all commoners and foreigners were required to leave the sacred valley several times a year when the Inca and his court performed special rituals.

The Incas had developed an elaborate system of knotted cords called *quipus*. These cords were made of the wool of the alpaca or the llama, dyed in various colors—the colors and various lengths of the cords signifying certain measurements. Knots were placed in such a manner as to represent the decimal system. The *rememberers*—the *quipucamayocs*, those who could decipher the quipus—recorded passing and current events. Most of the quipus were so complex only the rememberers could decode most of them.

When the Spaniards arrived, they ordered a census and each territorial governor sent quipus with detailed information. They included data about the number of people in each area, how many could bear arms, how many were of each gender, what was in warehouses, the success or failure of certain crops last year, who paid what in taxes, and who fought who and how many were killed or injured.

During the conquest the Spaniards destroyed vast storehouses of quipus, burning not only the public records, but all the personal archives in an effort to stamp out the pagan religion of the Indians. But they could never destroy the quipus engraved in the hearts of the Incas, many of whom still worship the sun on Inca feast days and festivals. But most of the quipucamayocs have long since passed from the scene. Few can decode the simplest quipu today.

No one knows the origin of these Peruvian Indians over whom the Incas ruled. Perhaps they are the result of some ancient migration. But one can only speculate as to the direction of the migration. One can assume that the entire race descended from a Quechua tribe— but whence came *that* tribe? The skin of the Quechua was brown in color. Their hair was straight and black. Seldom did one see gray hair among them. Seldom did one observe a beard. One seldom saw a bald head or false teeth except on a sugar plantation. The men still wear their hair long and braided.

An overweight Indian among the Incas was extremely rare, perhaps because their diet contained very little fattening food such as meat. Their diet

consisted mostly of white potatoes, corn and *quinoa*—
a plant similar to our beans, which was their protein.
They had very few meat animals, since both llamas
and alpacas were never regarded as food animals.

Bachelors were seldom found among the Incas but
polygamy was practiced only among the upper classes. The Inca rulers, the military leaders and the nobles
were usually awarded concubines. They were called
Chosen Women—and were taken from national convents called *acllahuasi.* Once a year military leaders
and nobles sought out Chosen Women throughout
the empire. The women were trained in special duties.
Their lives were consecrated to the service of the sun—
the Inca ruler—his representatives, his priests and
his military leaders.

The Virgins of the Sun—their nuns—were totally
different from the Chosen Women. They dwelt only in
sacred convents. Guards were stationed at the door of
these convents, keeping guard over the aclla. They
were not allowed contact with any man and if such a
contact was discovered the temple virgin and her
paramour were killed. This is no different than the
lives of the vestal virgins in ancient Rome. There, too,
they were kept under guard and contact with any man
resulted in being buried alive in underground tombs.
The Mother Superiors of these Peruvian virgins were
called *mamacunas.*

A school for young noblemen called the *yachay-
huasi* was started by the Inca named Roca. The major
topics of study were Quechua, religion, history, quipu, geometry, astronomy and military instruction.

The walls of the school were decorated in a serpent motif because, to the Incas, as to so many other ancient cultures around the world, the serpent symbolized wisdom. Inca lads endured initiation rites very similar to those of North American Indians, that marked their entrance into manhood. The festivities, called the *huarachico*, were simpler among the peasants.

But in Cuzco—"The candidates, dressed in white, their hair cut and their heads wrapped in black *llautu* with black feathers, assembled in the great square where they addressed prayers to the Sun, the Moon and the Thunder. Then they climbed nearby Mount Huanacuari, at the same time observing the strictest fast (pure water and raw corn) as did their families. They took part in ritual ceremonies and dances, during which the priests handed them slingshots. A few days later, they received red and white tunics, and spent the night under a tent with their families at a spot near the capital. They afterward offered sacrifices, danced and took part in a race in the presence of a large number of Indians who encouraged them with their shouts."

The race was held under the sign of the falcon for its swiftness and nobility. The organizers of the race placed crude representations of animals—falcon, eagle, vicuna, fox, serpent, toad—at the summit. The runners grasped these representations as they raced by, the swiftest securing the falcon—the first choice— and the latecomers having to be content with the lesser choices. Each thus carried the evidence of his strength and his swiftness and the spectators applauded accordingly. Following the race, each young candidate carried a nickname that corresponded to the animal grasped during the race.

The day after the race, the young candidates were divided into two groups to attack and defend a fortified spot. The roles were reversed the next day and the battles resumed. After this, they applied their skills to the bow and arrow and next the slingshot before undergoing character tests. They were required to receive blows without complaining—as is often dealt to the Buddhist monks undergoing initiation. They were to serve as sentry 10 nights in a row without falling asleep, remain immobile while a club was brandished over their heads and their eyes were threatened with a lancepoint—no flinching.

After these tests they received the clothes, weapons and earrings of an adult knight. Piercing the earlobes with solid gold plugs was important and the piercing was repeated annually to stretch the lobe. An extended lobe was the mark of nobility and royalty. One remembers the massive earlobes of the grotesque statuary of Easter Island—and on many of the giant heads and forms at Tiahuanaco. The huarachico rites included ritual planting and harvesting at some of the holidays.

At Cuzco the entire week of June 24th, Peruvians and tourists by the thousands gather even today to witness the extraordinary Festival of the Great Winter Solstice, a reconstruction of the ancient *Inti Raymi* festival. This festival of the sun was almost certainly a pre-Inca ritual of initiation and in the Inca era all of the high level civil servants from throughout the empire flocked to Cuzco. Preparation for the festival included a rigorous three-day fast and all were forbidden to engage in sexual relations or to light a fire.

As the sun progressed farther and farther north during the month of June, it was the duty of the priests in the temples to observe the lengthening of the shadows. The priests constantly emphasized to the natives that they should fear the departure of the sun. Watching the shadows lengthening, the priests convinced the peasantry that only the high priests and the Inca himself could discover when the shadows had attained a certain length and that, if the priests did not tie the sun to a certain rock, it might continue its flight to the north leaving the peasants eventually to freeze and starve.

So it was that on the 21st or the 22nd of each June, the priests in a high religious ceremony stopped the sun in its flight by tying it to a stone pillar in one of their temples. Thus this pillar became a stone of great veneration. With the tying of the sun the shadows ceased to lengthen. They gradually became shorter until the sun was once more overhead, bringing great rejoicing among the peasantry. And the priests were held in great veneration for having performed so noble a deed.

"On the date set by the astronomers," writes Louis Baudin, "the supreme Emperor made his way to the central square before dawn. He found assembled there the members of the imperial *ayllu* (clan). In an adjoining square the *curaca* (bureaucrats) were grouped. All took off their sandals in utmost silence and turned toward the east, immobile, observing the horizon.

"At the moment when the streaks of dawn appeared to touch the summits of the *cordillera* (mountains) with gold, they crouched down, extended their arms in a gesture of supplication, and embraced the first rays. Then the monarch took a chalice filled with a sacred potion in each hand and, standing facing the rising sun, raised his arm above his head and offered the drink to his Father Sun.

"The sovereign afterward poured the contents of the chalice into a little duct which directed the liquid to the temple. (Part of the square contained a sewer system that permitted the libations poured into ceremonial basins to flow away or into the temple.) He himself took a mouthful from the chalice which he held in his left hand, divided the rest among the chalices extended to him by the people of his entourage, and requested everyone to drink. Then the members of the imperial ayllu entered the Temple of the Sun; the curaca followed them as far as the doors but remained outside.

"The supreme Emperor offered the Sun the two chalices he had used, and the onlookers presented theirs. Priests advanced toward the threshold of the edifice to receive the vessels from which the curaca had drunk and at the same time the presents which they had brought. The sacrifices began by putting to death a black llama, considered to be more perfect than any other because its entire body was of the same color, whereas the white llama had a muzzle of black."

Garcialasso de la Vega described a ritual which took place during this celebration which strangely recalls the Christian communion. The acllas prepared an enormous quantity of cornmeal dough, called *zancu*, for the Inca and made little round loaves of bread the size of apples out of it. Two or three mouthfuls were eaten at the beginning of the meal.

For another celebration, the Uma Raymi in October, two types of cornbread were prepared. The first, kneaded normally, was eaten at the rising of the sun. The other was prepared with blood taken from between the eyebrows of children from five to ten years of age. These rites seem even more bizarre because the Incas ate bread only during these two festivals.

The symbolic use of blood and the ritual of the Chalice is equally as astonishing to us today as it must have been to the Spaniards. It reminds one of the story told by the Tibetan lama, Lobsang Rampa, describing how a minute wedge of wood—no larger than a thin needle—was inserted between his eyebrows during initiation ceremonies to open his third eye. The use of bread and blood is still celebrated in most religions today—as the Holy Eucharist—the difference being that wine or grape juice is consumed as symbolic of the blood of Christ.

Cuzco in the background.

Another view of Cuzco reveals possible UFOs hovering
over the city while we were there.

Chapter Seven

The Immortal Incas

The word Inca correctly means king or emperor. The Inca in those ancient days was the chief whose genius guided his remarkable people to conquer most of Peru, Ecuador and Bolivia. The empire also included the northern parts of Chile and Argentina. In those days this vast territory was called Tahuantinsuyo—the Land of the Four Quarters. With the coming of the Spanish conquistadors in the Sixteenth Century the term of Inca was applied to the ruling class and his family. Also included were the nobles and priests governing the empire under the great chief Inca. Slowly the term Inca was used to include the entire race, which had built its incredible civilization.

Following the magnificent Manco Capac, the first Inca, each succeeding Inca was considered a king, an emperor, ruling over this vast territory. History speaks little of each until Huayna Capac, the son of Tupa Inca, became Inca.

Huayna Capac fathered over 200 children, five of whom later went on to become Inca. After many battle campaigns in his youth, he deserted Cuzco and estab-

lished a second capital called Tumipampa near Quito,
Ecuador in 1517. He returned to Cuzco only as a
mummy, following his death.

While Huayna Capac was living near Quito near
the end of his life, reports reached him of white
bearded men wearing silver jackets, wielding thunder
and riding four-legged monsters—and they could be
seen nearing the northern border. He immediately
consulted several oracles, none of which would prophecy for him, until he threatened to kill all the temple
priests and destroy the oracles.

He then received this message from the Pariacaca
Huaca—the one priest not cowed by the threats. *"It is
no longer time to speak of any government, for men
called Viracochas (white gods) will soon be arriving,
during your reign, to govern in the name of an all-
powerful lord."*

Huayna sent a message to Manco Inca, one of his
sons who would rule after his death: "Father Sun
revealed to me that after the reign of 12 Incas, his very
children, a kind of man would appear in our country
who would be unknown to us and who would subju-
gate our states. They undoubtedly belong to the same
people as those who came in times past from the
sea...Be assured that these strangers will arrive in this
country and that they will fulfill the oracle!" Shortly
thereafter Huayna Capac died in Quito of the same
plague that killed so many of his subjects.

But the Indians refused to accept this prophecy
and the wars which raged between the Indians and the
Spaniards lasted for 40 years, until the Incas were

finally vanquished. Huayna had laid the groundwork for future problems by building a second capital near Quito and for not naming his successor as Inca before he died.

The Coming of the Conquistadors

The leader of the Spanish invaders of Tahuantinsuyo (Peru), Francisco Pizarro (1478-1541), was an illiterate and illegitimate soldier of fortune. In 1513 Francisco was a 38-year-old officer accompanying Vasco Nunez de Balboa when Balboa "discovered" the Pacific. On July 26, 1529 the Queen affixed her signature to the document that endorsed Pizarro to proceed with the conquest of Peru as governor and commander-in-chief—but he had to finance the expedition himself. On his third expedition south from Panama, he finally acquired the men and the supplies needed to explore more than a narrow strip along the coast.

In September, 1532, Pizarro had finally reached the empire of Tahuantinsuyo with his men and supplies. He began his trek at the Rio Esmerelda—the Emerald River north of Quito. His younger half-brothers, Gonzalo, Martin de Alcantara, Juan, Hernando (the only legitimate and literate brother), and his cousin Pedro were part of the invading force. Another conquistador described the brothers this way: "...as proud as they were poor, and as much without wealth as eager to achieve it." More than any other individual, Francisco Pizarro was responsible for instituting widespread slavery in Peru.

When Huayna Capac died without naming an heir to succeed him as Inca-Emperor, Huascar, the first of his sons, was living in Cuzco. Hc was rightfully crowned the legitimate Inca. However, his half brother Atahualpa—who had lived in Tumipampa near Quito with his father—stayed there with all the hardened armies and experienced generals and named himself king of Quito. Thus there erupted a fierce battle between Huascar and Atahualpa as to which should be the supreme Inca. The entire country was split into factions, each acquiring many followers.

Huascar sent out untrained conscript troops from Cuzco against his insurgent brother. His troops were defeated near Ambato, Ecuador and Atahualpa ordered their skeletons stacked as a war memorial. Then Atahualpa ordered his trained soldiers to capture Huascar. These experienced soldiers fought their way south to Cuzco defeating all the inexperienced troops Huascar sent against them.

Although Atahualpa personally stayed in Ecuador and let his troops go into battle without him, Huascar finally decided to lead his troops himself. He and his troops met the rebel forces in a gorge at the top of the Apurimac valley and one of the bloodiest battles in Inca history followed. Chroniclers later wrote that over 150,000 Indians died. Huascar was winning early in the engagement, but made a beginner's mistake of stopping the battle for the night and celebrating his expected victory. Atahualpa's generals gathered their troops in the dark and waited to ambush Huascar and his troops the following morning. Huascar was captured and carried as a prisoner back to Cuzco.

Then Atahualpa's armies sacked Cuzco. They burned quipus and killed quipucamayocs. The quipus were the cords with knots which represented the only writings of the Incas and the quipucamayocs were the "rememberers" who could "read" the quipus and keep records of all the domestic and political happenings.

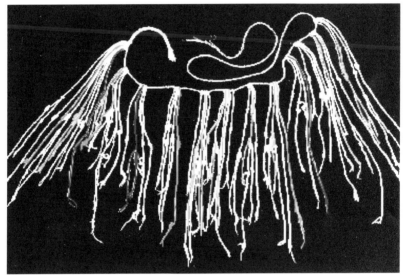

AMANO MUSEUM, LIMA

A quipu, a series of knotted strings used for record keeping. The strings were of different colors, thicknesses, and lengths to indicate different information.

They forced Huascar to watch the execution of his acllas (his Chosen Women) and his courtiers. Three of Huascar's sons managed to escape but Huascar as well as two other half brothers were assassinated. But the battle further divided an already divided nation. Many of the embittered populace refused to accept Atahualpa as Inca. Peru was a country in upheaval.

It was during this time that the Spaniards finally marched inland led by Pizarro. Atahualpa and his army of over 25,000 met Pizarro's ragtag band of 62 cavalrymen and 106 foot soldiers outside a small town called Cajamarca in northern Peru. The Inca and his entourage had stopped to enjoy the hot springs in Cajamarca on their way to Cuzco. Pizarro invited Atahualpa to join him for dinner in the plaza on Saturday, November 16, 1532. As Atahualpa had been promised that "no harm or insult would befall him," he came unarmed in his most splendid robes with several thousand of his followers.

When the Indians reached the square, a Dominican priest emerged from a building with a cross in one hand and a book in the other. The book was named "the Requirement" because the Spanish Crown had ordered that it be proclaimed before any blood could be shed in the conquest of a foreign people. The priest demanded that Atahualpa accept both Christianity and Spanish rule. After hearing a rough translation of the priest's speech, Atahualpa leafed through the book and then threw it angrily to the ground. He would not bend to another monarch nor kneel to a God crucified by his own people.

The priest then ran shouting, "Come out, Christians! Come at these enemy dogs who reject the things of God. That chief has thrown my book of holy law to the ground!" When Pizarro gave the signal cannons fired into the midst of the Incas and horsemen came charging, cutting down unarmed servants. The Spaniards climbed over piles of fallen Indians to reach the Inca who soon became Pizarro's captive.

When the killing frenzy ended, over 6,000 Indians were dead but only one conquistador was injured and none were killed. The Indians had kept their pledge of peace even in the midst of such heinous betrayal. None had raised weapons against the Spanish.

At this time, many of the people of Tahuantinsuyo believed Pizarro and his conquistadors were saviors who came in response to their prayers to Viracocha and Pacha Mama to rid them of Atahualpa. Many felt Atahualpa had an illegitimate claim to the throne and was a usurper. They prayed that these strangers would help resolve the problems he caused. The civil war he started with his half-brother, Huascar, was killing thousands of people, and the populace had not yet recovered from the plague that had decimated them only a few years earlier.

FROM THE ARCHIVES OF GENERAL INDIAS, SEVILLE

Francisco Pizarro.

Atahualpa—who also believed the Spaniards to be foreign gods—submitted to his captivity, and Pizarro permitted the Inca's subjects to serve him as they normally would. Pizarro demanded great hordes of gold from the Indians and sent shiploads toward Spain. He kept promising Atahualpa freedom for more and more treasure. Finally Pizarro offered freedom to the Inca in exchange for a 17 by 22 foot room filled with gold, and two more filled with silver. The Indians readily brought the required ransom.

But Pizarro refused to release the Inca even after he received his rooms full of gold and silver, declaring to the Coya (queen) that he would murder Atahualpa, her husband, unless the queen revealed where the vast treasures of the country were hidden. He demanded to know where the mines of gold and silver were located. He had also heard of the native Peruvian tradition that somewhere in the land there lay vast subterranean tunnels—chinkanas—extending many miles beneath the imperial dominions where the accumulated riches of the country were buried.

Not only legend but history describes how the beautiful queen begged for delay. In the meantime she fled to the inner Temple of the Sun in the Coricancha to consult with the oracles of the priests of the sun. Consulting their own oracles, the high priests requested that she look into the black mirror. This was a lamp-blacked magic mirror which the priests had prepared. The queen, gazing into the light of the black mirror, saw the fate of her Inca husband—murdered even if the tunneled treasures and the mines were delivered into the hands of Pizarro.

History records how the grief stricken queen ordered the underground tunnel closed forever. Such a closure was to be executed under the direction of the high priests and the magicians. Closed with the speaking of a certain code of words, only such a code could again reopen the tunnel. One can assume then that the treasure is lost forever since the entrance to the tunnel cannot be opened without the sound of the same magic words and the secret magical formula has long been forgotten. Those priests who knew it have long since died.

While imprisoned by the Spaniards, Atahualpa had over a hundred of his Chosen Women in captivity with him who were constantly humiliated by the Spaniards. Two of his favorites were raped. One, the beautiful Morning Star, committed suicide afterward rather than live with the shame.

If a Chosen Woman had shared the Inca's bed, it was a death penalty offense to sleep with a lesser mortal. Atahualpa cried out to the gods to transform the soul of Morning Star into a thunderbolt to strike down the Spaniard who had raped her and reduce his body to ashes. Three days later, while traveling to another city, the man was struck by lightning and killed.

Finally, the conquistadors decided that Atahualpa was too powerful. The rationale for his execution was to accuse him of secretly planning to order General Ruminahui to lead an army from Quito to free him. There was no trial but Atahualpa was informed of the charges—treason for putting an end to the truce and mobilizing to kill Christians!

On July 26, 1533, Atahualpa was brought to the square in Cajamarca, bound hand and foot. All morning Father Valverde had pressured Atahualpa to convert to Christianity. Finally he was told he would be garroted rather than burned if he accepted. Resigned to his fate, Atahualpa agreed. Pizarro's secretary wrote: "After he had pronounced his final words, while the Spaniards who surrounded him were reciting a credo for the salvation of his soul, he was promptly strangled." Three days later Pizarro announced that the rumor of an attack from Quito was unfounded.

At the time the queen ordered the tunnels sealed there were eleven thousand llamas loaded with gold and silver gathered from around the empire on their way to Pizarro's camp at Cuzco as a further ransom for Inca Atahualpa's release. When the Indians escorting the cache heard of the assassination of their Inca and the order of their queen to bury the treasure in hidden tunnels, the vast treasure vanished from the face of the earth. Only after learning that the treasure was buried did the despairing queen commit suicide to escape the fate of her husband.

Gaspar de Espinoza, governor of Panama, wrote a letter to Charles, King of Spain, praising Pizarro but decrying the execution: "They killed the Inca because they claimed he would have mobilized great contingents of warriors to attack the Spanish. Such is the reason which urged—let us go so far as to say forced—Governor Pizarro to act in such a manner; add to that the considerable pressure exerted upon him by Your Majesty's officers...

"In my eyes, it would have been necessary to establish and prove the Emperor's guilt by most formal proceedings, in such a way that no doubt could have remained, before even thinking of executing a man fallen into their hands and against whom no one, Spaniard or otherwise, felt the least prejudice. They could have brought him here to Panama, accompanied by his wives and servants as befitted his rank. The abundant ransom in gold had been provided to secure his release. We would have accorded him the honors he deserved and treated him with the same deference as a great lord of Castile. The more the Indian chiefs are inclined to give, the more the Spaniards strive to compel their own captains to kill or torture them in the hope of obtaining more..."

Pizarro did not fully realize that millions of Indians regarded Atahualpa, himself, as a god. It was he who had made their laws and controlled their very existence. But instead of rising in protest at Atahualpa's death, the Indians fell into a profound state of confusion. Millions of people fell under the control of that small company of invading Spanish soldiers. But they soon learned that the Spanish merely wanted to destroy their culture and steal their gold.

Later it was said that numerous omens were connected with Atahualpa's captivity and death. "The earth refused to devour the Inca's body—rocks trembled—tears made torrents, the Sun was obscured—the Moon ill." The plague which started during Huayna Capac's reign took 200,000 more lives, together with earthquakes, a green comet, and a lightning strike on the palace. Two condors killed a falcon (huaman), a quite holy bird to the Incas, in the sacred square during the Inti Raymi (Winter Solstice) festival. Also, the moon was seen on a clear night surrounded by a triple halo—the first ring the color of blood, the second black and the third like smoke. It was interpreted as: the blood announced the civil war between Atahualpa and Huascar, black signified ruin of the religion, and the end of the empire that would go out in smoke.

With both Huascar and Atahualpa dead, the Spaniards were storming the gates of Cuzco. Gods as strong as Inti seemed to protect the priests of the Coricancha from harm but the Willac Umu (High Priest) was in despair. He had already ordered that the sacred mummies of the Incas be relocated in the cordillera—the high passes and peaks—and ordered copies made of the Punchao and other treasures so that the originals might be buried high in the mountains. But how to protect the Virgins of the Sun, the nuns?

Almost as important as the gold and silver to the Spaniards were the Acllas, the Virgins, for they were bent on pillage and rape. They were astonished that the Incas considered the Virgins of the Sun much more important than the gold, silver and gems that adorned the temples and clothes of the upper classes. The Willac Umu consulted old quipucamayocs who told him that high in the mountains an untouchable city was built by the apus for the Sun so that the Incas would have a refuge in times of trouble. So the priest led the Acllas to the retreat of Machu Picchu. In their wake, all the bridges were torn down, the roads blocked and vipers released around the outer walls. Thus, Machu Picchu and the Virgins of the Sun were lost to time.

When the Spanish asked the people of Cuzco where the Aclla had gone they answered: "Father Sun took his Virgins to an inaccessible place so that they would not be attacked by the white foreigners."

El Dorado

After the Spaniards murdered Atahualpa and their queen committed suicide, the enraged Indians concealed a treasure consisting of from 600 to 650 tons of gold and jewels. To this day it has never been found. The value of this treasure is today beyond measure. Yet "they" say that this incredible treasure is no more than an ear of golden corn compared to the sum of the ancient subterranean treasures buried throughout South America, especially Mexico and Peru.

Treasure hunters from other lands, however, are still most cautious in their searches for such riches. Should they ever unearth it, most would be fearful to remove it from the country. There are still millions of Quechua Indians who revere the memory of Atahualpa and who would rise in revolt if such a plan was formulated. The Indians of old melancholy Peru still dream of the day when the wheel will come full circle and the vanished glories of the old Inca empire will shine once more over the land of the vanished Incas.

Quechua traditions believe these treasures lie buried in the Matto Grosso of Brazil and the jungles of Peru into which most hunters dare not enter. They may be buried in bottomless waterholes or deep in the heart of some overgrown lost city. Some of it may be

sealed in undiscovered caves. The Indians of today
have long since forgotten the secret. They do know,
however, that if all the gold that is buried throughout
these ancient lands were once again collected, the
quantity of it would change life on earth.

Pedro de Leon, writing in 1545 A.D. said: "If when
the Spaniards entered Cuzco they had not committed
other tricks and had not so soon executed their cruelty
in putting Atahualpa to death, I know not how many
great ships would have been required to bring such
treasures to old Spain, as is now lost in the bowels of
the earth and will remain so because those who buried
it are now dead."

Those of us who know of the vast network of
tunnels under Machu Picchu believe the enormous
cache of treasure was taken by the Indians to this
sacred city when Atahualpa was strangled and their
queen commanded the cache be concealed. That is
why Machu Picchu was and is called the lost *City of
Gold*—the El Dorado. These Indians, obeying the
command of their queen, fled with their loaded llamas
into the inaccessible heights of the Andes and buried
the treasures there—to be guarded by the priests and
the Virgins of the Sun. When these holy ones died,
their secret died with them.

The Last Four Incas

In *Everyday Life at the Time of the Last Incas*, Louis
Baudin writes: "The sovereign wore a sleeveless, knee-
length tunic, the *uncu,* a band of material that formed
breeches, and a long, wide cape decorated in geomet-

ric motifs which was thrown over the shoulders, the two ends being attached on the chest, or passed under the left arm and knotted over the right shoulder so as to free both arms. His vestments were of fine vicuna wool, his sandals of white wool. Ribbons encircled each leg above the knee and at the ankle. The insignias of power, the *mascapaicha*, consisted of one multicolored braid wrapped several times around his head above the forehead, from which hung the *llautu*, a red fringe with red tassels attached to little golden beads.

"In addition, three little black and white feathers from the sacred *corequenque* bird protruded from a large pompom which was at the highest part of the braid. His hair was cut short and his ears were stretched due to the weight of enormous disks of a precious metal. The members of the elite had the right to wear the llautu, but not a red one, and also ear pendants, but of a smaller dimension. Finally, a tooled bag filled with coca leaves hung at the monarch's side.

"In solemn ceremonies, the Emperor held in his hands either a golden scepter which was as long as a halberd, sometimes topped with small plumes, sometimes with the mascapaicha, such as when the Emperor wore a war headdress, or held a star-shaped golden club and a leather shield decorated with the imperial coat of arms."

Manco Inca—named after the first great Manco Capac—became the ruling Inca after the death of Atahualpa. In order to forestall rebellion, the Spaniards allowed the coronation of Manco II to take place with all the necessary pageantry after they conquered Cuzco in November, 1533. Pizarro told Brother

Valverde, the future bishop of Cuzco, to close his eyes to the pagan and idolatrous aspects of the ceremony. In front of thousands of Indians crowded onto the great square the new Inca made his appearance in an imperial litter. Behind him, in order of precedence, all the mummified monarchs had been placed in litters decorated with their coats of arms. The royal families and other nobles followed the mummies. The festivities lasted thirty days without interruption.

While making friendly gestures toward the Inca, the Spaniards systematically pillaged Cuzco's riches. Pizarro controlled the division of booty among his men and verified the profits for the crown of Spain, one fifth of the total take.

The young Inca had several reasons to be worried, but what is known of him shows clearly that he honestly did not realize the Spaniards' true intentions. Whereas the Inca's slightest gestures were immediately signaled to Pizarro by devoted spy-interpreters, the Incas possessed no information about the Spaniards. Traumatized by the civil war and blinded by his hatred of Atahualpa and the northerners from Quito, Manco did not understand right away that he was dealing with rapacious colonizers. In his eyes, the conquistadors had liberated Cuzco from Atahualpa's rule. Although certainly greedy, they seemed to let him take the reins of power, restore imperial prestige, and celebrate the ceremonies of the Incan religious calendar.

However, Manco's attitude gradually changed. First he learned that new foreigners were debarking regularly at San Miguel de Piura, and secondly, the "liberators" were behaving more and more like conquerors. Hernando Pizarro's campaign in Panama to recruit colonists had stupefying results. In a few months, Peru had become the goal of all the adventurers in the New World. The unrestrained rush for gold was driving the most impatient toward this new El Dorado.

The newcomers were unlike the first arrivals. Less disciplined than Pizarro's men, and distinctly more avid because they had not endured the hardships of their predecessors, the latest conquistadors undeniably contributed in a large measure in worsening the relationship between the Spaniards and the Cuzco aristocracy.

Although the conquistadors had been circumspect the first few months in Cuzco, this soon changed. The Spaniards still in Cuzco lost any curb on their excesses when Francisco Pizarro left to begin building Lima early in 1535. Juan and Gonzalo Pizarro, left behind to control Cuzco, were particularly hostile to Manco and he began to be continuously humiliated. Finally, when he rose up in protest, he was chained and displayed before his nobles. When he tried to fight when they raped his wives in front of him, they urinated on him. Criticizing the errors of the oracles who had preached submission he stated: "In truth, I say you are demons and not the followers of Viracocha, since you treat me thusly without motive."

When Juan and Gonzalo Pizarro left Cuzco in January, 1535, to join Francisco and the forces building Lima, they left Hernando Pizarro behind to keep order in Cuzco. During Holy Week in 1536, Manco Inca bribed Hernando to set him free just long enough to attend a religious ceremony in the Yucay valley, promising to return with solid gold statues of Huayna Capac for Hernando. Once free, he gathered an army of Indians around him and staged a revolt. His revolt should have been successful since the Spanish conquerors in Cuzco numbered less than 200. But he failed to reckon that due to conflicts among the Indians themselves, many were too frightened to follow him. They defected to serve the Spaniards, feeling that they were already conquered and fearing the Spanish weapons.

After a year-long siege, Manco and his troops fled Cuzco into the Urubamba valley. Manco took a massive bounty of treasure with him in gold and silver and extremely beautiful rich wool clothing. He also carried the Punchao, the removable center of the great golden image of the sun which had graced the principal mammoth wall of the Coricancha, the Temple of the Sun inside the walls of the fortress of Sacsahuaman. Three of his sons accompanied him, fleeing with their father into the Urubamba valley, one of the most inaccessible parts of the Andes.

Manco Inca and his troops made the mistake of pausing just before entering the inaccessible territory, to celebrate one last feast so that those who chose not to go with him into the highlands would have the opportunity to say farewell to those who were departing. During the festivities, many of Manco's soldiers became intoxicated. Thus, when the Spaniards swarmed upon them in a surprise attack, they were unable to reach their arms to defend themselves. The Spaniards recaptured much of the treasure which was being carried away from Cuzco. Manco Inca managed to escape with the Punchao, but the Spaniards captured his wife and his six year old son, Titu Cusi.

With the remnant of his army, Manco fled into the jungles and impassable passes to the top of a mountain. There he constructed Vitcos, his palace and his fortress. Using Vitcos as his base, Manco and his warriors struck often at his enemies who were unable to follow him into his retreat. He was often successful in battle against the Spanish because he had studied their weapons and tactics and used that knowledge wisely. For the rest of his life, Manco remained in exile, returning to Cuzco solely to kill the Spanish invaders.

After several years of tolerating Manco's raids, Pizarro finally formed an expeditionary force and sent it into the highlands to seek and destroy Manco and his fort. But being unfamiliar with such terrain it was easy for Manco's soldiers to ambush and slaughter almost all of the expedition. The survivors who straggled back to Cuzco told vivid stories of each disaster.

Manco Inca remained unconquerable until 1544 when Charles V became king of Spain. Charles sent a new viceroy with new laws from Spain. It was the duty of the new viceroy to establish these laws, among which was the edict to renounce Spanish holdings of the Indian serfs and return these lands to their original ownership. Compulsory personal service of the Indians was also abolished. There was every indication the Spanish crown was offering peace to the Indians, and it became widely known that the king himself did not approve of the cruel antics of the conquistadors led by Francisco and Gonzalo Pizarro.

Such reports led Manco to believe that he might appeal to the new viceroy for the return of his lost empire. He was eventually persuaded to do so and sent his letter to the viceroy via one Gomez Perez. Traveling with a dozen Indian bodyguards, Perez left Vitcos and presented the letter from Manco to the viceroy who received the news joyfully and immediately offered pardon to Manco and all of his refugees. When Perez returned to the Inca with this optimistic message, the Inca and his warriors prepared to depart Vitcos and return to Cuzco. But their departure was prevented by a tragic event.

The account of the event was told by Manco's son, Titu Cusi, who wrote an entire book about his father's life. He and his mother had escaped their captivity in Cuzco and rejoined Manco in Vitcos. But Titu, after spending several years in Cuzco, was familiar with the city, its weapons, its strengths and its weaknesses. He wrote the following:

"Because he did not like to be without me, my father sent to Cuzco for me and my mother. The messengers he sent took my mother and me secretly out of Cuzco to the town of Vitcos to be met by my father. There my father and I stayed for many days. At different times, seven Spaniards arrived saying that they were fugitives owing to having committed offenses against Pizarro and promising to serve my father with all their power for the remainder of their lives. They prayed that they might be allowed to remain in our land and end their days there.

"My father, thinking that they came with good intentions, ordered his captains to do them no harm for he wished to keep them as his servants. He commanded that they should have houses in which to live. My father's captains would much rather have put an end to them, but obeyed my father's orders. My father had them with him for many years, treating them very well and giving them all that they needed, even ordering his own women to prepare their food, their beverage and taking meals with them. He treated them as if they were his own brothers.

"After these Spaniards had been with my father for several years in Vitcos, they were one day playing at quoits with him (the Spaniards had taught the Indians various games such as quoits, bowls and chess). Playing the game was only the Spaniards, my father and me. I was then a boy about 15 years of age. In this game, just as my father was raising the quoit to throw, they all suddenly rushed upon him with knives, daggers and swords. My father sought to defend himself, but he was only one and unarmed and they were seven fully armed. He fell to the ground covered with wounds and they left him for dead. I being a little boy and seeing my father treated in this manner, wanted to go where he was to help him. But they turned furiously upon me and hurled a lance which only just failed to kill me also. I was terrified and fled among the bushes.

"They looked for me but failed to find me. The Spaniards, seeing that my father had ceased to breathe, went out of the gate in high spirits saying, 'Now that we have killed the Inca we have nothing to fear.' But at this moment the captain Rimachi Yupanqui arrived with some Antis (cannibal Indians) and presently chased them in such sort that before they could get very far along a difficult road, they were caught and pulled from their horses. They all had to suffer very cruel deaths and some were burnt. Notwithstanding his wounds, my father lived for three days."

Sayri Tupec

When Manco died, his eldest son, Sayri Tupec, became ruler and the next Inca. Sayri Tupec was totally unlike his father. One wonders if he was simply peace-loving or more fond of luxury and comfort than of making war. At any rate, he ruled quietly for ten years without warring upon his Spanish neighbors or displaying overt signs of hostility.

In the tenth year of his reign a new viceroy from Spain, Francisco de Toledo, offered movements towards further peace by contacting Sayri Tupec and offering him a life of peace and contentment in the Yucay valley, not many miles from Cuzco. The viceroy pointed out how much more comfortable the Inca would be living in this fertile and beautiful valley as opposed to the rigors of life in the inaccessible passes and jungles of the Vilcapampa. Many of the Inca's relatives were already living in Cuzco. Having access to these relatives, the viceroy selected them to act as ambassadors, issuing an invitation the Inca found difficult to refuse.

Even after signing the truce, Sayri Tupec lingered in his mountain kingdom because he still feared treachery. After months of deliberation, the young

Inca, surrounded by his high priests, held a holy ritual consulting the deities of their ancestors—Father Inti, Pacha Mama and all the sacred apus. They tapped into the huaca of the trees, the lakes, the rocks of the Andes.

To receive his answer, the Inca and his court entered a fast of several days. To seek the oracles of their ancestors required certain ceremonies. Extinguishing all fires, the procession toward the high peak began at dawn. There, before the stone idols, many animals were sacrificed. During these rites Sayri Tupec received his vision. He declared that the sun, the earth and the sky and all the apus advised him to return to Cuzco. Even at the cost of his life, he must return to the land of his ancestors, occupy his palace at Yucay and be recognized in the lowlands as the ruler he truly was.

All of the Inca's high priests decried his decision, reminding him of the treachery performed upon Atahualpa, Manco Inca, and so many of the royal family who perished at the hands of the conquistadors. Eventually, however, they must bow to the Inca's decision. Deferring to his determination to return to the lowlands, the high priests decided to accompany him in an effort to surround him with some measure of security.

The Inca was adorned with his royal garments. Around his forehead was fastened the crown of scarlet wool, fringed with gold tassels and topped with the three feathers of the mysterious sacred bird, the coriquenque. As a symbol of his rank the Inca carried a staff with two serpents twined around it. His coat of arms had the sun, moon and serpents displayed.

On October 7, 1557, Sayri Tupec, with his youthful bride, Titu Cuci, and over 300 of his loyal retainers departed the mountain fastness and his fortress at Vitcos. The entourage entered Cuzco on the evening of Epiphany, January 5, 1558. The litter upon which his faithful warriors carried him was draped with the most beautiful of his mountain fineries. The Inca and his procession entered the city with all the pomp and ceremony due a ruling Inca. A loud and festive welcome was rendered, designed to make him feel regal and acclaimed.

The Inca was led to believe that he would be given back much of his empire. The viceroy, however, insisted that he embrace Christianity, and marry an Inca princess of the royal bloodline. The Inca, already persuaded toward comfort and luxury, found the viceroy's plan enticing.

After a festive welcome both in Cuzco and Lima, Sayri Tupec returned to his palace in Yucay near Cuzco. He lived there in great pomp for about two years. Then he died suddenly under very suspicious circumstances. There was little doubt that he had been poisoned. Although the viceroy declared that the Inca died of disease, the nobles of Vitcos were firmly convinced he was poisoned. With his death, the crown of leadership passed to Titu Cusi, the favorite son of Manco Inca. Titu Cusi rejected life in Cuzco or Yucay and instead chose to return to life in the wilds of Vilcapampa. Enraged, he took up the battle cry once more.

Titu Cusi

Titu Cusi fled into the inaccessible valleys of Vilcapampa and assumed the throne of the Inca empire. Titu was about 30 years of age at that time. He sent his younger brother, Tupac Amaru, into Machu Picchu to dwell in the House of the Sun with the holy Virgins. Titu Cusi spent his life with his army at Vitcos.

It was at Vitcos that the viceroy again contacted the Inca to offer him luxury and comfort in Cuzco. The viceroy sent Don Diego Rodriguez de Figueroa as his ambassador. Figueroa left behind a most famous and lengthy narrative which tells of his journey into the wilds of Vilcapampa, and his attempts to persuade the Inca to desert his isolated valley and take up his life in Cuzco. He wrote:

"I left Cuzco on the 8th of April, 1565, after having received letters from Judge Matienzo to the Inca, Titu Cusi. With leave to make an entrance after having offered my services to go by that route, I went to sleep at Ollantaytambo where they gave me seven Indian carriers to show me the way.

"On the fifth day of May, ten Inca captains came to the suspension bridge over the pass of Panticalla. Richly dressed with diadems of plumes and lances in their hands which they brandished, and wearing masks on their faces, they came to the passage of the bridge where I was and asked me if I was the man who had the audacity to want to come and speak to the Inca. I said yes. They replied that I could not fail to be much afraid for if I felt fear I could not come because the Inca was a great enemy of cowards. To this I answered that if he was an elephant or a giant I might be afraid, but as he was a man like myself, I had no fear but I would offer him respect if he would let me enter under his word, I would do so for I knew that he would keep it."

For some reason Figueroa did not use the bridge to cross the Lucumayo river because his narrative continues to say that: "On the 6th of May I crossed the river in a basket traveling along a cable and seven Indians came with me. The ten Indians of the Inca helped me to cross and accompanied me. That night I slept at the foot of a snowy mountain. I set out on the 12th of May and went on to Vitcos where the seven Spaniards had killed the Inca, and their heads were still exposed.

"The Indians told me that those Spaniards had killed the Inca to raze the land and that they determined to kill him while playing horseshoe quoits. Juan Mendez did it with four or five stabs behind him until he killed him and to Titu Cusi, who is the Inca now, they would have done the same but he escaped down some rocks which they showed me. If they had wanted to kill some Indians they could have done so but their object was to kill the Inca. Then many Indians and captains assembled who seized the Spaniards and killed them.

"On the 13th of May I sent two of my Indians to the Inca with some refreshments of raisins, figs, and other things. The Inca received them well and gave them two baskets of peanuts which they were to take to me with a message that next day he would arrive so that we should see each other soon and that I need not travel further.

"On the 14th of May, the Indians of Vambacona had made me a large house on a strong height surrounded by entrenchments. Below were the houses of the inhabitants. The road by which he was to come was very clean and passed over a great plain. The 300 Indians with their lances and others from the surrounding country had made a great theatre for the Inca of red clay. They were awaiting his arrival and wished me to go out to meet him. They told me that the people of the village would wait on the plain and that they would show me a place where they had brought two loads of straw, half a stone's throw from the rest of the people. They told me to wait there and see the entry of the Inca and not to move until the Inca sent for me.

"Many lances were drawn up on a hill and messengers arrived to say the Inca was coming. Presently the escort of the Inca began to appear. The Inca came in front of all with a headdress of plumes of many colors, a silver plate on his breast, a golden shield in one hand and a lance all of gold. He wore garters of feathers and fastened to them were small wooden bells. On his head was a diadem and another around the neck. At his waist he wore a gilded dagger and he came in a mask of several colors.

"Arriving on the plateau where the places of the people were, he gazed where the sun was and made a sort of reverence with his hands which they called mucha (a kiss) and then went to his seat. There came with him a mestizo (mixed blood Spanish-Indian) with a shield and sword and in Spanish dress. He wore a very old cloak. Presently the mestizo turned his eyes in the direction where I was and I took off my hat. The Indians did not notice this. I grasped an image of Our Lady which I carried in my bosom, and though the Indians saw it they took no notice.

"Then two *orojones* (golden ears, nobles) came near the Inca with two halberds, dressed in diadems of plumes with much adornment of gold and silver. These made obeisance and reverence to the sun and then to the Inca. All the rest were standing near his seat, encircling him in good order. Presently the governor came, named Yamqui Mayta with 60 or 70 attendants with their silver plates, lances, belts of gold and silver, the same dresses that were worn by all who came with the Inca. Then came the Master of the Camp with the same gaily dressed following and all made obeisance first to the sun and then to the Inca saying, 'Child of the Sun, thou art the Child of the day.' Then they took up their position around the Inca.

"Then another captain entered named Vilcapari Guaman with about thirty Indians bearing lances adorned with feathers of many colors. Then came twenty men with axes, making reverence to the sun like the rest. All wore masks of different colors which they put before their faces. Next a little Indian entered who, after making reverences to the sun and the Inca, came towards me brandishing a lance and raising it with great audacity. He then began to cry out in Spanish, 'Get out! Get out!' and to menace me with his lance. Next, another captain entered named Cusi Puma with about fifty archers who were Antis—those who ate human flesh. Presently all these warriors took off their plumes of feathers and put down their lances. With their daggers of bronze and their shields of silver or leather or of feathers each one came to do reverence to the Inca who was seated and then returned to their places.

"Presently he sent for me and passing through that multitude of Indians I took off my hat and made a speech to him. I said that I had come from Cuzco solely to know and serve him. If I wore a sword and dagger it was to serve him with them and not to offend him. To this he answered that it was for men to bear arms, and not for women or cowards and he therefore held me in more esteem for that.

"But he said he was pleased at the trouble I had taken to come from such a distance to him, adding that he had come forty leagues only to see and converse with me. Then he gave me a cup of *chicha* asking me to drink it for his service. I drank a quarter of it then began to make faces and wipe my mouth with a handkerchief. He began to laugh, understanding that I did not know that liquor.

"The Inca was a man of 40 years of age, of middle height, and with some marks of smallpox on his face. His mien rather severe and manly. He wore a shirt of blue damask and a mantle of very fine cloth. He was served on silver and there were also 20 or 30 good-looking women waiting behind him. He sent for me to eat where he was with his women and his governor. The food consisted of maize, potatoes, and small beans and other products of the country, except that there was very little meat, and what there was consisted of venison, fowls, macaws and monkeys, all boiled and roasted.

"When night came on he asked me whether I had made the acquaintance of his captains. I replied in the affirmative and he then took leave of me. He went to the house that had been prepared for him in exactly the same order as when he arrived with music of silver flutes and trumpets. That night there was a guard of 100 Indians who were divided into watches, and flutes and drums were played to call each watch. They placed a guard of 15 Indians over me with their lances, I being in a house outside the village. I calculate that all the Indians who came with the Inca and those of the village numbered 450.

"In the morning of the 15th of May the Inca sent for me to come to his house for it was raining. The greater part of his troops were seated around a large fire. The Inca was seated dressed in a shirt of crimson velvet with a mantle of the same. All his captains had taken off the masks they wore on the day before.

"As daylight was now appearing and they had all drunk freely, I asked permission of the Inca to return to my lodging and get something to eat and that another day I would state frankly what I had come for. So I departed leaving them to boast loudly but all much disturbed in their minds.

"Soon afterwards, they sent me a sheep of Castile, (evidently the result of a successful raid on a Spanish colonial sheep ranch) many fowls and partridges, and other food which their country produces. To those who brought them I gave some trinkets, needles and other Spanish things. Presently the Inca sent for me. I went there and was there until night without a word being spoken when I returned to my lodging. The reason for this appeared to be that too much chicha had been drunk."

The Quechuas made it a ritual never to discuss agreements after consuming much chicha. Afterwards, Figueroa offered presents to the Inca. Beautiful materials, crystals, pearls, gold and silver jewelry. Then he asked permission to present a discourse on Christianity and asked permission to set up crosses as evidence of faith. But the Inca, instead of being pleased, reacted angrily and loudly proclaimed he had a good mind to order him killed. Figueroa continues:

"From the top of a rising ground, I saw the festivities made for the Inca and heard the songs. The dances were war dances with spears in their hands, throwing them from one to another. I believe that they did such things by reason of the quantity of chicha they had drunk.

"The Inca sent for me late in the afternoon and I went against my will. He told me to sit down. He then began to boast that he himself could kill 50 Spaniards and that he was going to have all the Spaniards in the kingdom put to death. He took a lance in his hand and a shield and began to act a valiant man, shouting, 'Go at once and bring me all the people that are behind those mountains for I want to go and fight the Spaniards and kill them all, and I want the wild Indians to eat them.'

"Then there marched up about 600 or 700 Antis Indians, all with bows and arrows, clubs and axes. They advanced in good order, making reverence to the sun and then to the Inca and took their positions. Then the Inca again began to brandish his lance and said that he could raise all the Indians in Peru. He had only to give the order and they would fly to arms. Then all these Antis made an offer to the Inca that if he wished it, they would eat me raw. They said to him, 'What are you doing with this little bearded one here who is trying to deceive you? It is better that we should eat him at once.' Then two renegade Inca orojones came straight to me with spears in their hands, flourishing their weapons and saying, 'The bearded ones. Our enemies.' I laughed at this but at the same time commended myself to God. I asked the Inca to have mercy and protect me. So he delivered me from them till morning.

"On the morning of the 16th of May the Inca sent for me to come to the open square which he entered in the same order as before, and as I came in I saluted the Inca and sat down. The Inca and all the captains then began to laugh heartily at what had happened the day before and they asked me what I thought of yester-day's festival. I replied that I thought it rather exceptional and that to have treated me so was wrong, seeing that I had come on serious business. They explained that it was only their fun and that they could not give it up. Then the Inca permitted me to set up a cross near his encampment. Then the Inca invited me to make my report. I told him of the might and power of Charles V of Spain.

"To this he replied that the power of the king was great, and though he had so many nations as well as black men as Moors subject to him, yet he, the Inca, like Manco Inca, his father before him, knew how to defend himself in these mountains.

"Presently, he sent to Vilcapampa villages for more men, who were savages arriving with bows and arrows, coming to impress me. On the 25th of May, one of his generals arrived with 300 men armed with lances who entered the open place where the rest were drawn up and made obeisance to the sun and to the Inca. Then 100 captains of those who came from the wilds of the Vilcapampa mountains went to where Yamqui Mayta was standing and asked why he had consented to have the cross planted in their land seeing that it had not been set up in the time of Manco Inca. Why then was it there now? If I had persuaded the Inca to do this, they intended to kill me. The Inca replied that it was done by his order and that it was well that they should accept the cross of the creator of all things. Having received this answer, they went to their seats and the festival proceeded."

Having delivered his invitation with great courage and bravery, Titu Cusi appeared to be almost persuaded to follow in the footsteps of the previous Incas and leave Vitcos to live in comfort in the Yucay valley, not far from Cuzco. Nevertheless, Figueroa returned to Cuzco without the consent of the Inca.

The viceroy, however, was not totally persuaded that the Inca would never come to dwell in Yucay. So he again dispatched Figueroa to seek another audience with the Inca. However, this time, 30 Spanish soldiers and a number of Indian guards were sent with Figueroa. When Titu Cusi caught sight of this armed force attempting to cross the bridge at Chuquichaca he became so alarmed he ordered the bridge torn down, sending Figueroa and all the Spanish soldiers back to Cuzco.

However, he chose from among the Spaniards one Martin Pando to act as his secretary, since the man spoke both Spanish and Quechua. Martin Pando lived in Vitcos for the next five years, winning the confidence of the Inca.

Martin was able to convey to the Inca that Charles V had abdicated in Spain to be followed to the throne by his son, Philip II in 1565. Because of this change, Martin suggested it might be wise to adopt Christianity and appeal to the new king, Philip, to recognize his right to wear the sacred fringe of Inca sovereignty and to have at least a part of his empire restored to him. Martin also suggested that he might welcome several of the Christian monks into the fortress of Vitcos. With Martin acting as his secretary, the Inca began a correspondence with Don Lopez Garcia de Castro, the governor of Cuzco. Eventually, Titu Cusi wrote:

"Having received letters from your Lordship, asking me to become a Christian and saying that it would conduce to the security of the country, I inquired of Diego Rodriguez and Martin Pando as to who was the principal monk among those who were in Cuzco, and who were the most approved and of most weight among the religious orders. They replied that the most flourishing were those of St. Augustine and their Prior was the most important priest in Cuzco.

"Having heard this, I became more attached to the order of St. Augustine than any other. I wrote letters to the Prior, requesting him to come in person to baptize me, because I would rather be baptized by him than by anyone else. He took the trouble to come to my country and to baptize me, bringing with him other monks, a Gonzalo Perez de Vivero and Atilano de Amalya who arrived at Rayangalla on the 12th of August, 1568. Wither I came from Vitcos to receive baptism. There in that village of Rayangalla were the said Prior named Juan de Rivero and his companions. I was instructed in the things of the faith for a fortnight. At the end of which time, on the day of the famous St. Augustine, the Prior baptized me."

During the baptismal ceremony the Inca was given the Christian name of Diego, which was the family name of governor de Castro. His godfather was Gonzalo Perez de Vivero and his godmother was Donna Angelina Zica Ocllo.

"After I was baptized the Prior remained for eight days to instruct me in the Holy Catholic Church and to initiate me into its mysteries. He then departed with Gonzalo Perez de Vivero, leaving me a companion named Friar Marcos Garcia, that he might little by little instill into my mind what the Prior had taught, that I might not forget. And also to teach the word of God to the people of my land. Before he departed, I explained to my followers the reason why I had been baptized and had brought these people into my land.

All replied that they rejoiced at my baptism and that
Friar Garcia should remain."

A Spanish chronicler, Father Calancha, takes up
the story from there:

"It was the year 1556 that the Father Friar Marcos
Garcia took up residence behind the walls of the great
Inca sanctuary called Vitcos. He set to work to fulfill
his mission of educating the Inca to the mysteries of
Christianity and to save the souls of any Indians that
came under his persuasion. He built a small church
two days' journey from Vitcos and set up many crosses
in the territory."

After some time he was joined by Father Friar Diego
from Cuzco, sent there by the governor of Cuzco.
Perhaps he was sent because Father Marcos had been
unable to make much of an impression on Titu Cusi.
Because of his failure to convert the Indians he was
ready to depart and hoped that Friar Diego could
replace him. The Indians came almost immediately to
love Friar Diego since he had a totally different person-
ality from Friar Marcos. Friar Diego made it clear that
he had not come to replace Father Marcos but had
indeed come to build a second church apart from
Marcos Garcia. Apparently the two priests were not
filled with brotherly love.

Titu Cusi gave him permission to build the church
a distance of two or three days' travel from the church
of Friar Garcia. Along with his church, Friar Diego
built a hospital with the help of the Indians who were
anxious to please this gentle medical missionary.
Because of his kindness, his anxiety to teach the

Indians, to cure them and to clothe them, the Indians began deserting their own religious sites and seeking the Christian community.

Meanwhile, Friar Marcos fared no better than before. He was constantly persecuting the Indians for their beliefs, rebuking ancient superstitions and scolding the Indians for their habits, especially those of Titu Cusi and his nobles. This, of course, did not endear him to the Inca. Finally he decided to depart the province and return to Cuzco, becoming instinctively aware that he had aroused such hatred among the Indians that his life was no longer safe. But the Inca learned of his departure and sent five of his captains to find him wandering through the wilds of Vilcapampa and brought him to Titu Cusi's encampment. Once there, the Inca demanded an explanation of his departure from the province without permission. Whereupon, Father Marcos prudently replied:

"Señor, the Indians whom you have in this pueblo do not desire to receive the faith, nor to hear the word of God. They run away from me and insult the holy doctrines which I preach to them, most of those who requested baptism being already enemies of Christ, our Creator. If your Indians had received the faith, or if those who did receive it had not apostatized, I would remain among them till death. Those who now accept the faith and are baptized are Indians who came from Cuzco; others fear to come to me."

Having somewhat abated the anger of the Inca he was told to return to his church. Shortly thereafter, Titu Cusi decided to take Friar Marcos and Friar Diego on a foot journey to his "capital seat" of Vilcapampa because they were constantly seeking a converted Indian to show them the way. (This, of course, would have been Machu Picchu which no Spaniard had ever seen.) The Inca and his nobles departed on the journey with the two priests with the deliberate purpose of making the journey so hazardous as to discourage any future attempts to find and invade the sacred city. And that is exactly what happened. Subjecting them to the perilous journey not only was an attempt to discourage them from ever seeking to find Machu Picchu, but to encourage them to leave the province and return to Cuzco.

The chronicle of Father Calancha describes this part of the journey: "They came to a place called Ungacacha and there the Inca and his nobles perpetrated the infamy that they plotted, which was that they covered the roads with water, the country being inundated by turning the river from its course. The Friars desired and had often attempted to go to the city of Vilcapampa (Machu Picchu) to preach, because they said it was the chief town and the one in which was the University of Idolatry and the professors of witchcraft, teachers of the abominations." (Which proves how little the Spanish priests truly knew of the religion of the Indians, their rites, their initiations and their Mysteries.)

"The Inca, in order to frighten the Friars so that they would not attempt to live or preach in Vilcapampa, but would leave the province, plotted a sacrilegious and diabolical scheme. Shortly after daylight on descending to a plain, the monks thought that they had come to a lake. The Inca said to them, 'All of us must pass through this water.' Oh cruel apostate! The Inca did not take his Christian baptism seriously as the monks wished he had. He traveled in a litter and the two priests on foot without shoes. The two monks went into the water and proceeded joyfully, as if they were treading on fine carpets, for they knew they were receiving these insults and torments because of the Inca's hatred of their preaching.

"There, in extremely cold, waist-deep water, they were chilled through and through. Cold and covered with mud they came out on dry land and there the Inca told them that he had come by that difficult route because he thought it would so disgust them with the attempt to settle in Vilcapampa that they would go from thence to Cuzco."

Titu Cusi brought the Friars only to the outer vicinity of Machu Picchu (Vilcapampa) and left them there to ponder whether or not they would ever desire to make a return journey. The Inca was determined the Friars would never preach inside Machu Picchu, the principal seat and sacred city of Vilcapampa. But even in the outer vicinities, the monks immediately began preaching and attempting to convert the Indians. They also became aware that this hidden city, now called Machu Picchu, was a great sanctuary. They could only catch glimpses of magnificent rooftops. But Titu Cusi made very sure they caught no sight of the beautiful buildings themselves.

When Titu Cusi became aware that, in spite of all his injunctions against it, the two priests began preaching and attempting to convert the Indians on the outskirts of the province, he and his nobles became extremely upset. To distract the Friars from their fervor, Titu decided to dictate to them the account of the life and death of his father, Manco Inca.

On completion of the account, Titu Cusi returned to his palace in Machu Picchu, but the account had so aroused the curiosity of the two Friars they decided to secretly invade the sacred city. They hoped to witness some of the festivals of sun worship, which they felt to be the height of paganism. Having gained entrance to the sun temple, Friar Marcos and Friar Diego gathered around them some of the Indians they had succeeded in converting, with the intentions of burning up the devil they were convinced dwelt in the temple.

Among them were those faithful to the Inca who came to witness how their own god could defy the devil of the Christians. To carry out their rites, the two monks piled great stacks of firewood throughout the temple of the massive rocks. There, they began their exorcism to vanquish the devil, calling him by every vile name imaginable and demanding that he depart, never to return. The fire, of course, rose beyond their control, burning the temple completely and scorching the massive rocks. The Friars claimed success, however, declaring they had caused the devil to flee, never to return.

When Inca Titu Cusi and his mother learned of the incident, they and the nobles were enraged. They sought to kill the missionaries, but were persuaded to pardon Friar Diego and focus their wrath only upon Friar Marcos. He was stoned out of the province and threatened with death should he ever return. Friar

Diego was so beloved by the Indians that Titu Cusi came to forgive him and finally accepted him as a friend and advisor.

It was through this friendship that Father Diego eventually persuaded Titu Cusi to accept an invitation of his cousin, Carlos Inca, who dwelt in Cuzco, to attend the splendid christening of his son. The ceremony was attended by all the ranking Spaniards and Indians of the vicinity of Cuzco. Several accounts state that the Inca was persuaded to attend this ceremony, whereas several others deny it. It cannot be denied, however, that Father Diego won the esteem and respect of the Inca, after Father Marcos had departed. But Titu did not attend the ceremony.

The climax to the drama unfolded when Titu Cusi planned his annual pilgrimage to the place where his father, Manco, had been assassinated. His priests and followers and two monks accompanied him. During the festivities honoring his father, the Inca imbibed great quantities of chicha. At the height of the festivities he suddenly collapsed in great agony in full view of his priests and two wives. His body suddenly swelled and turned purple and he began to cough up blood. One of the Christian monks—Diego Ortez— rushed to his side offering a remedy—an egg beaten with sulfur and red pepper. He persuaded the reluctant Inca to drink the remedy and a few seconds later, struck by paralysis, Titu Cusi died amid agonizing spasms.

Instantly, one of his wives—Coya Polanquilaco— attacked the monk, accusing him of poisoning her husband. She demanded he revive the Inca with a mass to prove his innocence. Titu Cusi did not revive.

The enraged Indian priests fell upon Ortez. Stripped naked, he was placed upon a cross, his arms were broken, and he was forced to spend the night hanging on the cross in the freezing cold. The next morning he was scourged and dragged with a rope before the new Inca, Tupac Amaru, the younger brother of Titu Cusi. Furious because the monk had loudly reproached Titu Cusi for his vices and his sins, Tupac Amaru sentenced the monk to death. After five days of fiendish agony, Ortez was finally slaughtered.

It was decided that Titu Cusi's death would be kept secret from the Spaniards in Cuzco who kept sending emissaries to persuade the Inca to come from the highlands and give up his prolonged isolation. Each of the messengers disappeared until finally no messenger could be persuaded to climb the high mountains to issue the invitation.

The Indians were filled with grief and sorrow, expressing their fury over Titu Cusi's death with death dances and loud cries and wailing. The litter bearing the Inca, decked with scarlet fringe and shield, carried in the hands of the greatest lords, was followed by a long procession of mourners. The procession continued into Machu Picchu where Inca Tupac Amaru waited in the House of the Sun. Tupac Amaru became then the true and legitimate lord of the Incas. It is presumed that Titu Cusi was buried at Machu Picchu.

Chapter Eight

Tupac Amaru, the Last Inca

So it was that in 1571 Tupac Amaru, the third of Manco's sons, became ruler of the province of Vitcos. Meanwhile, the Indians had discovered that the new viceroy, Don Francisco de Toledo, had no tolerance for the Indians' customs, religion, or way of life. He reinstated the slavery that the Pizarros had instituted. He seized every opportunity to display his displeasure and react with cruel punishment. He was a fanatic who brought all of the terrible excesses of the Inquisition to Peru.

Unaware that Titu Cusi had died or that Father Ortez had been executed, the viceroy dispatched a trusted ambassador to the province of Vitcos to invite the Inca again to come to dwell where he would fall under the domination of Spanish authority. Even though news of happenings in Vitcos was slow to reach the Spanish authorities in Cuzco, news of the new viceroy and the events in Cuzco reached the ears of Vitcos very rapidly.

Thus the Indians learned that the invitation to the new Inca was on its way long before it ever reached Vitcos. They warned the new Inca about accepting the invitation. They reminded him that Sayri Tupec had been poisoned while dwelling in comfort and luxury at Yucay near Cuzco. They reminded him too that Manco Inca had been murdered by Spanish refugees, even while he was befriending them. They reminded him that Titu Cusi had died while being ministered to by Father Ortez.

They felt it was necessary to issue these warnings to the young and inexperienced Tupac Amaru. They feared for him to leave the security of Vitcos to go to live at Cuzco. They determined to stop the ambassador on his way with the invitation and to execute him. So that the young ruler would not be involved in the execution, they persuaded him to journey into the warm valley of the Pampaconas, where his older brother, Titu Cusi, had built a country home near the savage Antis Indians before he died.

When the viceroy, de Toledo, learned of the execution of his ambassador and, at the same time, of the martyrdom of Father Ortez, he was enraged. Believing he had no other recourse, he ordered war upon Tupac Amaru and offered a reward to any soldier capturing the Inca. The reward was one thousand Indian pesos a year for two lifetimes. He was determined that the Inca royal family be terminated.

Together with his rage was the hope that by the imprisonment of Tupac Amaru he, the viceroy, could find the lost Inca treasure of El Dorado including the magnificent chain of gold and the golden medallion which the great Inca Huayna Capac had worn on royal occasions. He knew too that the treasure included the renowned golden Ark of the Covenant—the Punchao—which once had graced Coricancha, the Temple of the Sun inside the great walls of Sacsahuaman.

He issued an edict that these treasures—the gold medallion and the golden Ark, the Punchao—belonged to King Phillip of Spain "by right of conquest." The main expeditionary force chose the route that led them to the Chuquichaka bridge where, 35 years earlier, the well-trained soldiers of Manco Inca had slaughtered the Spanish soldiers. The expedition was led by Martín Garcia de Loyola, the nephew of Ignatius Loyola, the founder of the Jesuits. (Ignatius Loyola was the spirit guide of Dr. John (Joâo) Texeira in Brazil who performed psychic surgery on my eye in the clinic of Abadiana.)

The conquistadors fully expected the bridge to have been destroyed as it was before. But the young Tupac Amaru, having had no experience in warfare, left his chieftains to defend the bridge. All were unaware that the Spaniards had brought with them several light mountain guns which the Indian troops had never heard before. When the Spaniards sent rapid gunfire into the mountains across the bridge, the Indians panicked and fled in terror, leaving the bridge undefended.

Loyola and his troops crossed the bridge and began their conquest into the highlands. He destroyed everything in his path, Indians by the hundreds and every fort along the way. Tupac Amaru finally retreated into the fortress of Vitcos. Loyola constantly reminded the Indians along the way of their incredible reward for the capture of the young Inca. One of Tupac's staunchest generals, Puma Inca, tempted by the compelling offer, decided to desert Tupac and lead Loyola to his secret hideaway—Vitcos. Joining forces with Loyola, he sketched a map of the fortified slopes, guiding Loyola directly to the fortresses and retreats of Tupac Amaru.

As Loyola approached the well-fortified stronghold of Vitcos, his strong heart was dismayed to view the single entrance. The gateway was barely wide enough to admit one person. Not quite ready to admit defeat he again sought assistance from the Indian traitor. Puma Inca advised that while the Inca's forces concentrated on defending the entrance, Loyola and his men might enter via an almost unused slope, assuming that Tupac Amaru would not bother to guard this forgotten side. Puma Inca was right. Loyola and his men were successful and the fortress fell, but Tupac Amaru had learned of his comrade's betrayal and departed the night before. Tupac's warriors and captains fought valiantly, sacrificing themselves to delay the Spanish troops, enabling Tupac Amaru and a troop of his soldiers to make their escape, carrying with them the golden Punchao.

Tupac with his loyal commanders fled toward the green hell of the impenetrable *paititi,* the wild Peruvian jungle, with the Spanish army following close behind. A few of the Indians among Loyola's troops sought Tupac in the mysterious city of Machu Picchu. But when they entered they faced a sore disappointment. Expecting to find stupendous treasures of gold and silver, all they found was a city occupied by women and children and a few old people. Gone was the Inca. Gone was the gold and silver and even the prized Punchao. In the Royal Mausoleum, the soldiers found the mummies of several famed Incas. The mummy of Manco Inca gazed out at them like a victorious ghost.

The Indians were so fearful of the wrath and reprisals of the gods, they would not defile the mummies and fled the city. Tupac, with his best captains and 80 Indians had already escaped to the east. The deadly and mysterious Andean jungle of the Matto Grosso was inhabited by savage tribes of Indians, wild animals, impenetrable woods, unmentionable insects —an unknown death land which only the brave dared venture. Even the haughty Loyola hesitated to follow, but the vision of the famous golden idol of the sun, the Punchao, danced before him and he refused to give up the chase.

Fearing the wrath of the viceroy back in Cuzco should they return without the Inca and the Punchao, Loyola and his troops followed Tupac relentlessly through the jungles. He was finally found at the foot of a massive tree, cradling his pregnant wife in his arms. She could go no further and he refused to desert her. In surrendering, he truly felt he might be taken into Cuzco and offered a dwelling at Yucay as had been done for previous Incas. But he was doomed to disappointment.

Tupac Amaru, the last of the incomparable line of the Incas, was bought back to Cuzco with a chain around his neck, led like a dog to the great plaza. When the Indians were told he was to be beheaded, they put up such a storm of protest the Spaniards hesitated for several days. But when the protest bordered on violence, they hastily carried out the execution. There in the great plaza, amid the wails, tears and cries of the Indians, the last great Inca was beheaded.

Atahualpa strangled and beheaded—Manco Inca stabbed—Sayri Tupac and Titu Cusi poisoned—Tupac Amaru decapitated. The forty-year war was over. With the capture and execution of the last Inca, little is known of what happened to the sacred Ark of the Covenant, the Punchao. When the Spaniards first landed, it was removed from Sacsahuaman at Cuzco and hidden in various temples. The Spaniards were never able to capture this priceless treasure, although they claimed they had. Keeping it out of their hands was the main reason the wars continued. The massive disk itself which covered one wall of the Coricancha could never have been carried from temple to temple and hidden forever from the Spaniards because of its enormous size. But the several Centers could have— the laser Arks and the Oracles—especially the Punchao.

The most important Center—the Punchao, the Ark of the Covenant—was the prize that the gold-hungry Spaniards wanted most of all. It was the oracle through which the Indians claimed to speak to Viracocha, Lord Maru, Manco Capac and Mama Occla. It had supernatural powers, executing miracles never before seen on earth. To send it to the Court of Spain could be the greatest accomplishment of any Spanish soldier, gaining historical fame for himself and his country. Even a small part of it would bring a lifetime of riches to any of the mercenary soldiers following Pizarro. The Ark of the Covenant, hidden at Machu Picchu when the Spaniards first landed, was the Center which Tupac Amaru was attempting to save when Loyola overtook him on the edge of the Peruvian jungle. It was this golden "Center"—the Punchao—which Loyola boasted of capturing. But it was the Punchao itself which utterly vanished.

Although Tupac and his wife were captured, the captains who fled with him were not. They would never have fled into the deeps of the jungle leaving the Punchao behind with Tupac and his wife. Obviously they took the Punchao with them into the jungle of Matto Grosso when Tupac Amaru decided to cease fleeing and remain with his exhausted pregnant wife to be captured by de Toledo.

Being familiar with the network of tunnels throughout the country, the captains surely would have entered one to escape Toledo and his troops—and to hide forever the sacred Punchao. They had no choice but to leave Tupac behind when he refused to leave his beleaguered wife. They too believed Tupac would be pardoned to dwell in the warm valley of the Pampaconas. Instead, the infamous Toledo was to commit one of the most heinous acts of the Inquisition—the beheading of the last Inca.

It has never been made clear what actually became of the Punchao. Was it taken into Machu Picchu when the Spaniards first arrived to be carried away by a spaceship—to prevent it from falling into the hands of those who, not understanding its nuclear and laser power, could destroy Peru and its people?

Was it carried deep into the Peruvian green hell of the Matto Grosso by Tupac Amaru and his captains and hidden forever in the impenetrable tunnels? Or did the Spaniards actually capture it and send the Ark to the Pope who hid it away in the secret archives of the Vatican? This is extremely doubtful because no further word about its capture has ever been mentioned. If it actually had been, the report would have rung throughout the world. The priests and scientists worldwide would have demanded that it be placed on public exhibition that all the world might know of its powers to communicate with aliens from a distant planet and to share in the miracle of such a happening. Or, using the cosmic rays of the Ark to overcome gravity, Spain could have levitated enormous stones to create pyramids, temples of worship, or anything else they chose. Or was a Center actually captured by the Spaniards which was only a facsimile of the original, without the power of the original?

For four centuries, its whereabouts have remained a close-guarded mystery. However, many are certain—at least hopeful—that the secret has been handed down through the generations so that there may be at least one living Peruvian who knows the location of this magnificent golden symbol, a reminder of the glory days of Peru. It is the last holy relic of a vanished and incomparable race.

It is believed by mystics to be hidden in the Matto Grosso where it will one day be found—just as the lost chambers of the Great Pyramid will one day be found. It is believed that one of the tunnels under Machu Picchu leads directly to the tunnel in the jungle where the ancient golden communication center is hidden. Perhaps it will only be discovered when those space beings who communicated through it to those in the temples of Machu Picchu return—the Builders of this lost El Dorado, the City of Gold.

Chapter Nine

The Tunnels of Peru and the Treasure of El Dorado

Hiram Bingham, writing a book describing his adventures and his discovery of the Lost City of the Incas, declared that the city of Machu Picchu had lain deserted and forgotten for four hundred years. During the conquest of Pizarro, the Incas had rescued their Temple Virgins from the approaching Spaniards who were bent on pillage and rape.

With their rescuers, the Virgins of the Sun had fled to a city lost among the peaks and mists of the mountain of Machu Picchu. The Incas called it Vilca-pampa because it was surrounded by the wilderness of the Vilcapampa jungles and rivers and because the sacred vilca plant grew on its slopes. Their route led them through a mysterious tunnel dug under the bed of the Rio Urubamba—a tunnel so secret its existence was not known until 1894. It was discovered then by an explorer named Vejar Ugarte and his guide, Augustine Lizarraga—the same guide Hiram Bingham would hire 17 years later on his search for the Lost City of Gold.

Ugarte and Lizarraga, having discovered the lost tunnel, never revealed its exact location and covered its entrance. They determined that the secret passage had been used for the purpose of routing the Virgins of the Sun to the hidden city of Machu Picchu centuries before. Having covered its entrance it was again lost until 1930. The re-discoverers found it fascinating that this was the only access at the time to Machu Picchu—those brilliant bridgemakers had never created a rope bridge to span the Urubamba at this important point at the foot of the sanctuary. No one has ever known who the original builders of the tunnel were. It can only be assumed to have been built during ancient times by those who built Machu Picchu, for the purpose of leaving the mountaintop city and descending into the lowlands without having to cross the wild waters of the Urubamba.

There are reputed to be thousands of miles of tunnels all over South America. Stone and metal objects of different colors and sizes have been found in caves and tunnels throughout.

Many feet below the surface, at the northern end of the Inca empire, there are tunnels with smooth walls, right angles, flat glazed ceilings—they resemble modern bomb shelters. Compasses won't operate inside them. Metal plaques (leaves) engraved with signs and writings—only millimeters thick—stand without buckling. In one chamber that is 153 by 164 yards (which are the same dimensions as the Pyramid of the Moon at Teotihuacan in Mexico) there is a table with seven "chairs." The chairs don't really look or feel like metal or wood—they seem to be some sort of plastic. Many different animals of molded metal are arranged behind and around those seven chairs.

In those same tunnels were found gold objects that archeologists have said were birds or fish. However, no fish or bird cult has been found in the area. An aeronautical engineer, Dr. Arthur Poyslee, has said: "The possibility that the artifact is meant to represent a fish or bird is very slight. Not only because this gold model was found deep in the interior of Columbia and artists would never have seen a saltwater fish, but also because one cannot imagine a bird with such geometrical wings and high vertical fins." The artifact has been tested in wind tunnels and is aerodynamically flyable; and it looks like the modern jet, the Concorde.

One of the enormous subterranean tunnels beneath Machu Picchu runs directly into Cuzco. All along the way in these tunnels there are tremendous slabs blocking the way and only by speaking secret formulas of sounds will the stone slab pivot on its axis and open to admit further passage through the tunnels. They extend throughout Peru into Bolivia and perhaps even into Brazil.

In 1971 an expedition sponsored by the magazine "Bild der Wissenschaft" went into caves that Pizarro had found closed with rocks. The expedition found watertight doors made of stone slabs that *could* be opened. Although heavy, four men were able to open the slabs because they pivoted quite precisely on stone balls.

"Vast tunnels, which would leave even modern underground constructors green with envy, began behind the 'six doors.' These tunnels lead straight towards the coast, at times with a slope of fourteen percent. The floor is covered with stone slabs that have been pitted and grooved to make them slip proof. If it is an adventure even today to penetrate these fifty-five to sixty-five mile long transport tunnels in the direction of the coast and finally reach a spot eighty feet below sea level, imagine the difficulties that must have been involved in the Fourteenth and Fifteenth centuries in transporting goods deep under the Andes to save them from the grasp of Pizarro and the Spanish Viceroys.

"The Great Ocean lurks at the end of the underground passages of 'Guanape,' so called after the island that lies off the coast of Peru here, because it is assumed that these passages once led under the sea to this island. After the passages have gone uphill and downhill several times in pitch darkness, a murmur and the strangely hollow sounding noise of surf is heard.

"In the light of the searchlight the last downhill slope ends on the edge of a pitch black flood which is identified as seawater. The present day coast also begins here underground. Was this not the case in former times?"

Now who could have built this mysterious tunnel in the first place? Certainly not the Incas during the days of the Pizarro conquest, although they obviously knew of their existence.

Helena Blavatsky, founder of Theosophy, during her journey to Peru in the years 1851 and 1853, declared there were landmarks cut into many of the peaks in the Andes pointing the way toward hidden tunnels. But they were only visible when the sun struck the cliffs at a certain angle, exposing the inscriptions of the secret code. The entrance to the tunnel would open only if the inscriptions could be properly interpreted and the words of the secret formula spoken.

She was told that these mountain landmarks could be found near the Rio Tayquina in Arica and that there was a hidden door in these mountains. This was said to be the only accessible door to the immense underground corridor extending between Cuzco, Lima and Bolivia containing various caches of gold, gems and jewels. Almost a hundred years ago she wrote;

"We had in our possession an accurate plan of the tunnel, the sepulcher, the great treasure chamber and the hidden, pivoted rock doors. It was given to us by the old Peruvian (the one who spoke of the hidden door near Rio Tayquina). But if we had ever thought of profiting by the secret it would have required the cooperation of the Peruvian and Bolivian governments on an extensive scale—to say nothing of the physical obstacles.

"No one individual or small party could undertake such an operation without encountering the army of brigands and smugglers with which the coast is infested and which, in fact, includes nearly the entire population. The mere task of purifying the mephitic air of the tunnel not entered for centuries would also be a serious one. There the treasure lies, and tradition says it will lie 'til the last vestige of Spanish rule disappears from the whole of South America."

The same old Peruvian who told Madame Blavatsky about the secret tunnels also told her of his consuming hatred toward the official Peruvians and the conquering Spaniards. He swears his hatred is shared by a great number of his countrymen even today. "I keep friends with them, these banditos," he said, "and their Catholic missioners for the sake of my own people. But I am as much a worshipper of the sun as if I had lived in the days of our murdered emperor, the Inca Tupac Ameru.

"Now, as a converted native and missionary, I once took a journey to Santa Cruz del Quiche (in western Guatemala). And when there, I went to see some of my people by a subterranean passage leading into a mysterious city behind the Cordilleras (high mountain peaks). Herein it is death for any white man to trespass."

Madame Blavatsky professed belief in the old man's story because, said she, "A man who is about to die will rarely stop to invent idle stories." The old Peruvian spoke of an historian called Fuentes who lived around 1689 A.D. In an unpublished history of Guatemala, Fuentes tells of these underground tunnels and of a long-vanished race. He says "the marvelous structure of the tunnels, of the pueblo of Puchuta, being of the most firm and solid cement, runs and continues through the interior of the land for the prolonged distance of nine leagues (twenty-seven miles) to the pueblo of Tecpan, Guatemala. It is proof of the power of these ancient kings and their vassals."

The Peruvians of today still remember Atahualpa and his betrayal. They remember Tupac Ameru and his flight from Martin de Loyola. They remember they were both beheaded. They believe the captains who fled with Tupac vanished into a great tunnel east of Cuzco leading into the dreaded jungles—taking with them the golden Punchao, the center of the magnificent sun symbol of the Quechuas through which their ancestors, the Sky Gods, spoke to their Inca Emperors. They speak of this underground civilization as the Gran Paytite.

The old Peruvian said that in these lost inner world cities, hidden behind the cordilleras of the Andes, dwell these emissaries from an ancient civilized race. They dwell there in the same majestic palaces and temples, massive courts and lofty towers as did their ancestors. The old Peruvian, speaking to Madam Blavatsky, told a story that happened in his youth.

He declared he had seen with his own eyes a mysterious lost city. He said the padre of the little village near the ruins of Santa Cruz del Quiche had heard of this unknown city when he was in the village of Chajul (Chajul lies in the mountains in western Guatemala close to the headwaters of the Rio Usamacinta). The priest was then a young man. With much labor he and the priest climbed to the naked summit

138 LOST EMPIRE OF THE GODS

of the topmost ridge of the sierra of the cordillera. When reaching the height of ten or twelve thousand feet they looked over an immense plain extending toward Yucatan and the Gulf of Mexico.

At a great distance they saw a large city spread over a tremendous space with turrets white and glistening in the sun. The old man told Blavatsky no white man had ever reached the city. The inhabitants spoke the Maya language. They knew that strangers conquered their whole land and they murder any white man who attempts to enter their territory. They had no coin, no horses, no cattle, mules or other domestic animals except fowls.

The story of hieroglyphics carved high up into the cliffs of the Andes to point the way to tunnels reminds me of hieroglyphics found in our own land. In the Grand Canyon of the Colorado there are arrows cut into the sheer walls which can be seen only when the solar rays strike certain angles of the cliffs. One wonders to what destination they are pointing—if we followed those arrows, would we find lost cities and buried temples? Perhaps a vast treasure brought by Montezuma when he fled into the deserts of Arizona?

I remember a site here in Southern California we discovered not long after we arrived in Los Angeles in 1951 to open our center called Astara. It was a place known as Harmony Grove, an enchanting little Spiritualist Camp between Los Angeles and San Diego, not too far from the city of Escondido. These Spiritualists were known for their Sunday services which attracted many people from the surrounding areas. They came because well-known psychics presented seminars and lectures. Also one could enjoy a marvelous Sunday lunch or dinner in their large cafeteria.

But of fascinating importance to me was that on the side of a sheer cliff rising at one end of the small area were mysterious hieroglyphics. These unique carvings covered the entire upper face of the cliff. Did they point toward a secret entrance to a tunnel? Did they speak of buried treasures? What were the architects of these carvings trying to leave behind for those of us in the present generation?

I'm sure similar writings and carvings could be found throughout the Southwest of the United States, except that those exploring them attach no significance to them and, after viewing them curiously, turn away wondering and then forget, as I did.

All the Indians of Peru know quite well that even should a secret tunnel be discovered today under Cuzco or Sacsahuaman or some other ancient fort or city, they would not be apt to find the long sought treasure tomb of El Dorado. Those who created the tunnels were well aware there would be grave robbers and treasure seekers. Again, great slabs were placed throughout the tunnels to block the way of those who lacked the "open sesame" secret words to turn the stones on their pivot. And should they apply dynamite to force an opening, they well know the entire tunnel would collapse, burying the treasure and the treasure seekers.

Tunnels Throughout the Planet

Tunnels in the Caucasus Mountains (the republics of Georgia and Azerbaijan) are believed to connect with tunnels that stretch to Iran, Afghanistan, Western China and Tibet. They are said to look almost exactly like tunnels found in South America. In Turkey there is an underground city thirteen stories deep with doors of giant stones which could be locked from the inside to close the shafts.

Tibetan Buddhists fervently believe there are vast tunnels under the massive monastery of Lhasa, former home of the Dalai Lama. They just as fervently believe they lead to a magnificent city underground called Agharta or Shamballa, where an ancient tribe of people dwell who escaped the cataclysmic Deluge that destroyed much of surface Earth. The leader of these ancients is called the King of the World and the people expect him to emerge one day to rule the world.

Tibetans believe these underground citadels once gave protection to the last survivors of the great cataclysm. Their legends state that these inner earth survivors were said to use an underground energy source that replaced the sun. It gave a green fluorescence that enabled plants and animals to grow and helped to prolong human life. Curiously, a report from South America about some tunnels there states the tunnels were lit "as though by an emerald sun."

The Apache Indians of the American Southwest tell stories of tunnels between their homeland and the city of Tiahuanaco in Bolivia. These tales report that many of their ancestors traveled these routes for many years until they reached South America. The tales also say that the tunnels were "carved out by rays that destroy living rock," and that the ones who dug them were "beings that live near the stars."

The Apache name for the god of light and fire was Ammon-Ra and, without prompting, they described a statue of a bearded white man that stood in Tiahuanaco. They say the god holds a sword upright in either hand, at right angles to the forearm, to signify "friendship within limits." Also that the place where the statue stands is the ancient home of their tribe. Could Tiahuanaco be the birthplace of North and South American Indians? It reminds us of the enormous stone statue there in Tiahuanaco called Ra-Mac. Was Egypt involved?

There are many tales of spacecraft in East Indian literature. The most probable location of the "Cape Canaveral" of the ancients is a ghost town on the Deccan plateau in south central India. This city is accessible only through a steep tunnel that runs from the base to the summit of the mountain—just as such a tunnel runs through the base of the mountain of Huayna Picchu near Machu Picchu and extends to the summit of Huayna where the hierophant sat to observe initiation ceremonies taking place below on the summit of Machu Picchu and the stone of the Intihuatana. I'll describe it in full later.

Secret tunnels have been whispered about throughout the world. Almost everywhere I have traveled, guides and other natives in the land have spoken furtively of hidden tunnels and secret entrances. I found two in Egypt and one in the Yucatan. The

Buddhists, as I've said, say that one city of that inner world is called Shamballa. Another is Agharta. Buddhists say that another entrance to Agharta-Shamballa is in the Gobi Desert.

A race of space gods, called the Annunaki, and their offspring the Nephilim, are supposed to have once known of this vast land, reached only through tunnels which radiate throughout the planet. And from the poles are supposed to come some of the UFOs now invading our skies. I spoke much of the Annunaki and the Nephilim in one of my other books.* Some equate the lost world of Agharta-Shamballa with the lost Shangri-La.

Supposedly this inner earth race of people are those who escaped the tremendous cataclysm that destroyed Atlantis. The legend—if it be a legend—says they lived not only on the earth's surface but also in a paradisiacal world beneath the surface. They lit their cities with the strange lighted crystal stones I shall describe in Chapter Eleven. The tunnels were also thus lighted.

When I led a tour into the Yucatan in 1982, our splendid guide at Uxmal, Chichen Itza and Palenque spoke of mysterious underground people and the lost tunnels, especially during our stay at Palenque. There, the walls of the temples and the canyons are replete with hieroglyphic writings. There, too, not only our guide but other natives spoke of people that suddenly appear in the pueblos and townships of the Mexican frontier state of Chiappas. They vanish again as suddenly as they appear.

*Revelations of Things to Come available from your bookstore or from Astara, 800 W. Arrow Hwy., Upland, CA 91786

Back in the early 40's, before I ever became so seriously interested in mysticism, lost worlds, hidden tunnels, UFOs and such esoteric subjects, I heard the story of a couple named Lamb. President Franklin Roosevelt had invited this husband and wife to the White House to hear the story of their contact in the state of Chiappas with a strange Indian tribe called the Lancandones.

This tribe spoke to the Lambs of a lost Mayan city behind a pass in the high mountains of the Yucatan. They described a city and a magnificent temple whose walls, plastered with gold plates, bore hieroglyphic writing telling of the history of the world and predicting World War Two. It also told of the great Deluge and catastrophe that destroyed Atlantis. The Lambs related this story to President Roosevelt and the story appeared in news releases. Stories such as this underscore the belief that there may be more than one "lost" city in the dense and unexplored jungle territory of the Yucatan.

The Indians of Chiappas tell of other dead cities hidden in the vast jungles and ranges of the Yucatan, protected by the rising cliffs and cordilleras. In these temples hieroglyphic writings may be found, recording the history of the antediluvian times. One wonders how, even today, the lost cities and the secret tunnels may play a part in the lives of the Quechua Indians who dwell in Peru, Yucatan, Guatemala, Chiappas and Ecuador.

Do they still remember Viracocha and Quetzalcoatl who arrived with the Sky People so many centuries ago?—who walked their lands and spoke of peace and love, who taught them agriculture, writing, astronomy, home building? Do they still enter the secret tunnels on their special days of the year and hold their secret ceremonies of worship in the dead cities behind the weathered rocks and cliffs of the cordilleras? Do they still wait for Quetzalcoatl and Viracocha to return and establish once again a golden age of light?—as we wait for Jesus?

I remember how I looked forward eagerly to my visit to the Cave of Loltun in the Yucatan. Loltun means "flower in stone." I had heard of an old priest who lived in a city deep in the earth. Occasionally—perhaps a couple of times a year—he wandered to the surface through the entrance of the Cave of Loltun to visit two brothers who dwelt on the surface.

Robert Stacy Judd in one of his books tells of his contact with this old priest during one of his journeys into Mexico. He and five other explorers entered the vast Cave of Loltun stringing along behind them their rope by which they would find their way to the surface again. Somehow the rope became lost among them and they found themselves wandering deep in the cave utterly lost.

For hours they wandered about throughout the vast tunnels, going first down one tunnel and then another, seeking the one which led to the surface. They seemed to become even more and more lost. They were on the verge of giving up and submitting to starvation and death in an underground cavern when suddenly, from deep inside the earth, at the end of one of the tunnels, there appeared a strange light. Nearer and nearer it came until they could determine that it was carried by an aged, blind man.

The light he carried was a mysterious sort of lamp. He told them he knew they were lost and that he had come to lead them back to the surface. Following gratefully, they once again emerged to the light of day. They discovered the aged person to be an old priest who had become blinded because his eyes were never exposed to the sunlight. They inquired of him how he could possibly survive deep in the bowels of the earth. He simply replied, "My friends take care of me." Then he turned and vanished once again into the cave.

Being familiar with this story I was most anxious to reach the Cave of Loltun. There I began questioning the villagers who dwelt near the cave and especially those who had set up a small center from which to sell their wares to the tourists. I inquired eagerly concerning the aged priest who occasionally came to the surface. At first they eyed me quizzically and then began speaking rapidly between themselves in a language not familiar to me. They then told me they had an older relative who might remember the old priest. They called the relative and asked him to come speak to me. When he arrived he spoke readily of the story.

He told us he did remember the old priest and that he did indeed appear at the surface of the cave occasionally. He did come to visit two of his brothers who still dwelt on the surface. Blind as he was to our world he could "see" much better than could the surface people when in the deeps of the cave. There his sight was quite keen—through the inner sight of clairvoyance. His stay on the surface was brief and he always insisted on returning to his subterranean home to join again his "friends who dwelt below."

The Mexican gentleman reporting this story to me said the blind old priest had died about twenty-five years earlier. When I asked him how he knew of the death of the old priest—since he had lived so far underground with his "friends"—he said his brothers had found his body one day lying in state just inside the entrance of the cave. Apparently his friends had borne his body up to the surface so that his brothers might know of his death and could dispense with his body as they saw fit. How else could his dead body have arrived at the entrance to the cave? Who were his friends dwelling below? In what city did they dwell? What manner of light did he carry in his hand?

How did he know of the six lost explorers in the cave above his city? So many questions—so few answers.

My Personal Belief

I should make clear my own personal beliefs about the inner earth civilizations. I am certain there are tunnels extending throughout the planet—but I do not believe there are actually people living today in the inner cities that once existed there. I believe the cities *were* occupied in the distant past, but I believe those who dwelt there have long since departed earth.

I *do* believe there are bases just inside the openings of both the North and South Poles—landing bases for

Kabah—the old priest who said he lived in an inner earth city.

The entrance to the endless tunnel inside the Cave of Loltun.

UFOs. I believe surface dwellers *did* enter the tunnels and dwelt in inner cities during and following the Deluge that destroyed many surface cities. I think those inner cities are now lying as lost as Machu Picchu was for 400 years.

I hope I shall prove to be wrong and that we shall one day learn of inner earth cities and their inhabitants—because I believe them to be advanced beyond us. Always when I have decided such can't be true, another "something" happens that causes me to believe again—like the story of the blind priest. Perhaps some adventurer will one day find one of the cities, as Bingham found the Lost City of the Incas. I think he'll find them probably as empty as Bingham found Machu Picchu. Those who built them have vanished—as all the ancient Builders vanished. Quien sabe.

Chapter Ten

Hiram Bingham and the Lost City of the Incas

When Hiram Bingham, the modern discoverer of Machu Picchu, wrote his own book concerning his discovery, he quotes Rudyard Kipling as his source of inspiration. *"Go and look behind the ranges—something lost behind the ranges. Lost and waiting for you. Go."* He declares that these words kept ringing in his consciousness throughout his adventure of seeking the Lost City of Gold.

Bingham was born November 19, 1875. In 1905, he began his quest, aspiring to follow in the footsteps of the unforgettable general, Simon Bolivar. Bingham began his trek by crossing the Andes from Venezuela to Colombia along the old Spanish trade route. He led another expedition out of Lima into Cuzco. The journey from Lima to Cuzco was made by a small train, jerking and coughing its way up the mountains to find Cuzco nestled among the mountains at an altitude of 10,500 feet. He rode on muleback into Cuzco which he immediately labeled "the navel of Tahuantinsuyo"—

the vast empire of the Incas embracing the impenetrable jungles of Brazil, the savannas of the Orenoque, the present countries of Bolivia, Ecuador and Peru and including Southern Colombia to the Rio Bio-Bio in the center of Chile. In the city of Cuzco even the peasants chatted eagerly about the legendary sacred lost city of the Incas, paved with streets of gold, topped with silver and gold roofs and statues of solid gold, encrusted with precious gems.

Bingham was aware that in the previous 100 years three expeditions seeking the City of Gold had failed. Rumor concerning the Lost City became widespread as far back as the Eighteenth Century. But the first scientific exploration was led by Vicomte Eugene de Sartiges in 1834. De Sartiges failed to find the city. Another attempt was made by Leonce Angrand in 1853, and another by Samanez Ocampo, again in 1853. All these expeditions had failed to find the city. But the rumors concerning the City of Gold described temples, palaces, baths and enormous idols. El Dorado, the vast treasure of the Incas, was reportedly buried there. That's why the Lost City was called the City of Gold.

In 1909, Bingham and his party were entrenched on the banks of the Urubamba until a Chinese diver was disposed to dive into the torrents and swim to the other side carrying a coil of telegraph wires. These swimming jaunts enabled the Indians to improvise a footbridge which the mules, carrying the equipment, refused to cross. The men, carrying the heavy equipment and having to stop every 50 paces to catch their breaths in the high atmosphere, crossed the bridge

and made their way upward into a valley of enchant-
ment.

Another day's climb brought them to the city of
Choquequirao (Cradle of Gold), which they first considered to be the Lost City they so eagerly sought.
There the huaqueros—the natives traveling with Bingham—revealed their true objective for the expedition
by immediately dynamiting palaces and temples,
searching for the gold cache. Horrified at the destruction by the natives, Bingham went quietly about the
scattered ruins, measuring the bones of disturbed
mummies. Observing this action the Quechua natives, suspecting he was communing with the spirits
of the disturbed mummies, offered to help him in his
search. Perhaps the ghosts of the Sons of the Sun
whispered their secrets to Bingham, revealing that
Choquequirao was not the Lost City he sought.

Upon his return to Lima, his suspicions were
confirmed. Choquequirao was a frontier fortress, built
to defend the upper Apurimac Valley from the primitive tribes of the Chancas. There is little doubt too that
Manco Inca used Choquequirao as a retreat from
which to plan attacks against the Spaniards for eight
of the forty years during the conquest.

When Bingham declared that Choquequirao was
not the Lost City of Gold, the poor Quechua natives
were considerably surprised. Bingham could not accept the fortress as the Lost City because of the crude
construction of the temples and palaces. Also, de
Sartiges had camped at Choquequirao during his own
expedition and felt fully justified in believing that the
Lost City was buried elsewhere.

Bingham Led by Kipling

When Bingham made his second expedition in 1911, he seemed to have some strange intuition that he was traveling the correct route. Although he instructed his native carriers to question every native they met along their ascending route, he well knew he stood little chance of getting proper answers from the Quechuas.

News had spread through the entire mountain regions that an expedition was afoot seeking the Lost City. Certainly no native Quechua could be expected to give him proper directions. No white man was to be trusted. It wasn't that the Quechuas feared the travelers of the expedition—rather they feared the curse of the mummies that might be disturbed if the Lost City was found. Bingham was asking to be shown the way to the city of Viticos, or Vitcos or Vilcapampa la Vieja, because he knew not the name of the Lost City. But every Quechua questioned gives evasive answers.

Bingham did indeed seem to be led by the spirits of departed Incas. How else could he have known that the Lost City of the pre-Incas lay much further into the labyrinth of high granite peaks? The Quechua Indians, dwelling among the peaks and steep cordillera of the Andes had refused to reveal the precise location of the Lost City even under torture by the Spaniards. With the death of each of these Quechuas, the hidden city's location was forgotten and remained hidden for four hundred years.

Bingham's earlier expeditions, made in 1905 and 1909, should have discouraged this soldier of adven-

Hiram Bingham

ture. But Bingham was not a man to be discouraged. Besides, the ghost of Kipling kept whispering—"Something lost and waiting for you. Go!"

Remembering the finale of his previous expedition, when the Quechua dynamited Choquequirao, Bingham chose his native helpers most carefully for his 1911 expedition. He would not listen to any of their zealous advice. He seemed to already know exactly the route he must follow—seemingly led again by the whispers of the dead Incas. Bingham had only one unmistakable landmark in mind—a great white rock over a spring of water. Suspicious that every one of his zealous explorers would try to lead him astray—each of whom suggested different routes up the steep sides of the canyon—Bingham listened to no one. He set his sights upon one goal and nothing could deviate his journey. He seemed to innately know the direction to travel.

The only point on which all the zealots enthusiastically agreed was that the name of the mysterious Lost City was Vitcos. But Vitcos appeared on none of the ancient or more modern maps, even those as late as 1865. Some of the Indians described Vitcos as two day's journey from Vilcapampa, others three. But where was Vilcapampa? All agreed that the Lost City was the principal capital of the retreating, rebellious Manco and his warriors. Bingham seemed to instinctively know the route Manco Inca took when he escaped the hands of the Spaniards and fled with the imperial treasure—the golden Ark of the Covenant, the most important Center of the enormous Disk of the Sun which flanked the largest wall in the temple of the Coricancha at the fortress in Sacsahuaman—the Punchao.

Did he again hear the whispers of the Inca spirits?—and Kipling? In his own writings, he himself suggested as much. Now, wrote the historian, and only now would the spirits of the Incas allow the Lost City to be found. The trail Bingham followed was along the Vilcanota—the River of the Sun, sacred to the Incas—which eventually merges with the terrifying Urubamba, only to merge again with the Apurimac, and from thence into the mighty Amazon.

Bingham's expedition began its perilous journey in the cold winter of 1911. They were stopped on every hand by the turbulent "Lord River"—Apurimac. The wild current of this treacherous river cascades through the canyons, cutting a deeper gorge than the famous Grand Canyon of Arizona. This king of rivers together with the Urubamba took great delight in destroying all the liana bridges built by the tedious labor of the natives.

It was Manco Capac, the first Inca, who is said to have conceived the idea of building bridges of twisted maguey fibers. De Sartiges, crossing the bridges in 1834, described them as being constructed with ropes as thick as one's calf. They swayed in the breezes over the angry Urubamba.

Two hours out of Cuzco, the travelers began observing the andenes—the terraces on which grew lush fields of barley, wheat and corn. These carved agricultural gardens rose like step pyramids up the side of the canyon walls. The Quechuas claimed a deity for each of the incredible mountains of the Andes—the Salcantay, the Media Luna, the Huayanay, the Nudo Esquina and the Hatun Orcco. Each of these marvels rises to at least 18,000 feet. No good Quechua doubted that these deified mountains were eternally guarded by the Apus, the guardian spirits, the devas, the genies of the mountains.

Most of these monstrous mountains claim to have carved ledges and tunnels leading into secret caves, especially Salcantay, whose name means "the most savage." On the summit and ledges of Salcantay, say the Indians, dwells the god of the Andes, vacillating between the mountain's two heads. One of the heads—China Salcantay—is especially precious to the female deity. The other—Orcco Salcantay—is the king. Dwelling side by side they are recognized as eternal deities.

Perhaps even now long-deserted Lost Cities lie gracing the peaks of many of these giants. Certainly gigantic ruins of a lost civilization lie strewn along the summits of the turbulent Vilcanota river. Then there is Ollantaytambo—a city of mammoth ruins that date back prior to the Incas. Ollantaytambo lies like a giant ghost city at the entrance to a sacred valley. Once called Tambo, it must have housed the lords of a great civilization.

Even today it is still inhabited by their descendants. They declare that Tambo was created during the reign of Manco Capac, the first Inca. If this is true, the city could have been chosen as the site by one of Manco's brothers. The five brothers were sent out from Tiahuanaco in five directions to establish great centers of civilization. Just as Manco's staff sank into the earth to establish the site of future Cuzco, so could one of his brothers have thus chosen the site of Tambo. Certainly everything about Tambo points to a civilization preceding the Incas.

Turning back to his search for the Lost City, Bingham decided to travel the route previously opened by Eugene de Sartiges. Sartiges was a young diplomat at the French embassy in Rio de Janeiro whose adventurous spirit equalled that of Bingham. When he embarked in 1834 to make a perilous exploration through the Andes and the Amazonian jungles, he too sought the Lost City of Gold. The young Frenchman almost reached the foot of the Lost City before turning back.

Bingham, his men and his mules must have paused often to gasp for breath, so high were they ascending the mountain slope straight into the sky. He marveled at the ability of the Quechuas to plant their crops on the cascading andenes. How dismal must have been their lives in so destitute but magnificently beautiful canyons.

The leader of the carriers insisted on stopping to camp long before nightfall declaring that none of his carriers would travel after dusk because he who hears the wail or "banshee cry" of the god of the Willkamayo (or Vilcanota) after sundown will surely be stricken with *susto*, the "disease of sadness" and quickly die. The camp was laid on a ledge with a rugged cut which held some of the sleeping men. But most slept restlessly in the midst of the mists.

At sunrise, a wide, vivid, iridescent rainbow formed a bridge across the gorge of the raging Urubamba as if to invite Bingham and his carriers to cross. Through another torturous day this group of straggly, ill travelers struggled upward, coaxing their trembling mules along the narrow path leading ever higher. Despite his illness and discouragement, Bingham recorded that the majestic grandeur of the magnificent landscape was beyond compare.

But the expedition grew irritable. They had pushed through every kind of torture for twelve days since they departed Cuzco and had met with no ruins other than those scattered along the trail. Though some of them offered cities of palaces and temples, Bingham quickly asserted that none of them answered to the description of the city he sought.

Suddenly a tempest battered the peaks and the canyons, releasing rain, thunder, lightning bolts and rocks upon the terrified carriers. The natives huddled in fear and panic, convinced that the apus of the mountains were attacking them for leading the white man toward the Lost City. But Bingham faced the tempest stoically, still listening to the inner voice which whispered that he was approaching his goal.

With the break of a bleak, cold, gray dawn, it was discovered that the expedition party had camped on the property of an inn proprietor who was indignant that they did not seek his inn for rest and food. When he confronted Bingham and revealed his name, Bingham for the first time knew without a doubt he was on the trail of the Lost City.

The man's name was Melchor Arteaga and the site of the inn was Mandor Papa. This was the place and the innkeeper Hiram Bingham had been seeking since the day the expedition departed Cuzco. After being assured a monetary reward was forthcoming, he enthusiastically informed Bingham that a day's journey from Mandor Papa would bring the expedition to an entire deserted city resting on the peak of Machu Picchu.

Bingham, eager to push on immediately, was forced to curb his zeal as the tempest beat about them.

Regrettably he was forced to spend another night in the inn of Arteaga. The downpouring torrents turned to an icy drizzle by dawn, dampening the spirits of the travelers considerably. Above them, the peaks of Machu Picchu and Huayna Picchu lay covered with grey smoky mists.

Bingham, exhausted, disillusioned and discouraged, was for the first time filled with doubt as to the sincerity of Melchor Arteaga. He was hard-put to urge his native carriers to continue. Traveling with him were scientific companions, an engineer, a geologist and a doctor. All were totally convinced the Lost City simply did not exist and each urged Hiram to turn back. How could even a camp exist on such a peak, much less a city! Melchor Arteaga, who had promised to lead Bingham to the city, seemed to have changed his mind. He protested traveling in such dangerous weather.

Bingham discovered his real reason for protesting was because the native carriers had warned him not to betray an ancestral secret for a paltry sum of money. They had warned him of the wrath of the guardian apus who watch over the forgotten city.

But Bingham insisted Arteaga keep his promise. The gendarme traveling with Bingham threatened him with arrest should he refuse to carry out his promise. Reluctantly and filled with fury and fear, he led the party into the terrible green hell of the jungles blocking the way to the summit of the Picchu. The ground, soaked with days of rain, had become paved with deep mud causing the men to slip and slide as they struggled upward. The mud, rising to their knees, sucked around their feet and legs, often causing them to move forward slowly on all fours.

Suddenly the rain ceased and a blazing sun appeared, turning the jungle into a steam bath. The carriers progressed slowly, cutting away dense shrubs covered with long thin thorns which pricked the men like miniature swords. They entered the wisps of clouds surrounding the summits of the Picchu.

Finally, Bingham had had enough. He collapsed with exhaustion and disappointment. However, two treasure seekers who had recently joined the brigade assured him he was nearing the goal and urged him toward the city. They emerged on another ledge. There, before his eyes, instead of palaces, temples, baths and gold he beheld only a wretched, partially ruined hut. The two inhabitants and their families emerged from the hut fearfully to declare they had been hiding on the slopes of the Picchu for four years to escape the sergeants of the Peruvian army who constantly roamed the cordillera seeking to recruit Indians for the army. The wilderness of the Picchu was the only place they could find freedom from such military entanglement and also escape recruitment for workers in the vast agricultural establishments down in the valley.

Camped there on the ledge with his expeditionary force, the disillusioned, discouraged Bingham sat despondent, his dreams broken and dying. His only comfort was the incredible view of the world below. The sight dazzled even the imagination. It could have been breathtaking except that one's breath was already made difficult by the altitude. The entire entourage, sensing his despair, his fatigue, his quiet rage, his disillusionment, had drawn apart, leaving him with his thoughts.

Sitting alone, away from the expeditionary party, Bingham faced the realization of his shattered hopes. Where, where was the Lost City so many had promised him? How could they describe this dismal wretched hut as a Lost City? Where could all the gold have been buried? Where were all the palaces and the temples? He buried his face in his hands, giving way to total heartbreak.

Suddenly he felt a slight touch upon his hands. Lifting his face, he beheld before him a small Quechua boy, smiling, even laughing. The boy took Bingham by the hands. He knows, he said, where the City of the Inca is. Bingham stared at him incredulously. How could a child know anything about the City of Gold? He almost pushed him aside, asking to be left alone. But before Bingham could voice his protest, the small lad pulled him to his feet, assuring him he knows the way to the Lost City. Reluctantly Bingham rose, too weary to withdraw his hands.

The small lad led Bingham forward and around a bend, circling a massive white boulder, and pointed toward the summit of the Picchu. Bingham almost collapsed with astonishment.

There before his very eyes stretched the grandeur, the stupendous glory of the Lost City! There before him were the temples, the palaces, the baths, the magnificent walls and remnants of the hanging gar-

Machu Picchu—the Lost City of Gold—the El Dorado.

dens. Just as suddenly, the sun broke through the mist, flooding the entire summit with golden shafts of sunbeams. At first Bingham thought he might be surveying a mirage rising out of the mists. The Quechua boy assured him this was indeed the Lost City of the Incas.

After recovering from his shock Bingham jumped on a thick wall to run toward the city. A huge overhanging rock blocked his way. Under the rock he found his second shock. The overhanging rock formed a cave. He could only assume the cave to be a *Royal Mausoleum.* The entire wall was lined with niches deep and tall enough to hold a standing mummy. Tiers of benches around the walls created an arena of the room. Benches were carved in the rocks so that those observing the funerary or spiritual rites might meditate or chant—or just watch.

The Torreon.

Leaving the mausoleum, he explored the horse-shoe-shaped *Torreon* above it. Bingham compared this strangely shaped building to a similar one found in the Coricancha, the famous solar temple in Sacsahuaman. He lingered awhile admiring the master work, declaring it to be the greatest piece of engineering and building yet found throughout all his travels in South America. It, too, was decorated with trapezoidal niches which lined the inner wall. Projected above the niches were strange quadrangular stone pegs, causing one to wonder what the inhabitants could have hung on them. Today, archaeologists still merely guess at their purpose.

Everywhere a magical miracle met his astonished eyes. The buildings again constituted temples, palaces, and baths. But there was no gold anywhere. If the temples and palaces were once topped with gold it had long since vanished. The treasures and gems of the Inca Kings—if they were here—were hidden away from the eyes of strangers. But it must have been there, somewhere. Else why did the ancients call this marvel the Lost City of Gold?

Everywhere monolithic stones were placed together to create the walls that will stand forever. Lines flowed in symmetrical beauty, graduating in places to end in gentle splendor, strengthening and becoming more powerful where needed. These stones too were joined without mortar, without the slightest gap.

The city is laid out in tiers, each level connected to the others by stone stairways carved into the rock or inlaid by granite slabs. Hundreds of steps connect the depths of the canyon with the summit on the highest peak (Huayna Picchu). Who could possibly have constructed such a site? How many were required to plan these carved walls?

This is the rock to which the ancient priests tied the sun during the Inti Raymi festivals each year. Even Bingham did not guess the summit was a temple of initiation. And it was a sun god —an initiate —not the sun, which was tied to the massive Intihuatana during initiatory rites.

Once again he beheld his little Indian guide. The boy, Mamani, beckoned Bingham to follow up the stone steps leading to the top of the highest pyramid in the city. There, at the very summit, surrounded by hanging clouds, he found mysterious *Intihuatana*, the stone to which the Willac Umu (High Priest) symbolically tied Inti, Father Sun, during the Great Winter Solstice Festival, the Inti Raymi. He pondered how this divine massive stone, carved to perfection, could have been elevated to such a height. From this summit he stood reverently surveying the entire sacred valley, the cone of Huayna Picchu rising nearby, and the entire Lost City sprawling at his feet.

The lad again took Bingham by the hand to lead him downward to the Temple of the Three Windows. These windows open out on a height to behold the entire region below for many miles distant. Set in a massive wall made of light-colored granite, they are unequalled anywhere in design and execution.

He was led next to what is now called the *Principal Temple*—three standing walls without a front that open onto a ceremonial plaza. Several impressive monoliths are found inside. One forms the great altar that must have been used for special ceremonies or to display mummies lying in state, because the enigmatic pre-Incan and Incan inhabitants did not perform human sacrifices.

Seeking his small guide once more, Bingham found him standing far upon the summit where the solitary Intihuatana Stone lay. The small lad refused to respond to Bingham's beckoning and calling. Instead he laughed as he did when he first appeared, and waved his hands in a happy farewell. Then he turned and walked directly off the summit to disappear into the void. The surrounding swirling mists immediatcly swallowed him up.

Bingham, rushing to the summit, callcd and sought frantically for the boy, but he was nowhere to be seen. Nor was he ever seen again. Who was this mysterious tiny sprite? Questions asked of everyone involved conveyed that he was known by no one, nor had he ever been seen in the vicinity before. How could he simply vanish into the void? Where did he go? Where did he come from? Why did he come? We who believe in UFOs believe he emerged from one for the sole purpose of leading Bingham to his greatest glory— otherwise the disconsolate Bingham might have given up his search when the Lost City lay just around a bend. Then, having accomplished his task, he re-turned again into the clouds which covered the wait-ing spaceship into which he entered and departed. Or,

The Principal Temple in the Sacred Sector.

others suggest, he was some guiding spirit sent from the higher realms of life to guide Bingham to this great discovery.

After completing several weeks of researching the entire city, Bingham departed to give the report of his find to those who had sponsored his expedition, Yale University. Having made his report he hurried back to his Lost City to find it even more impressive than before. The world press hailed him as a distinguished explorer and called the incredible discovery of Machu Picchu the most important event in the new world since the odyssey of Christopher Columbus.

Finding the city haunted him almost as much afterward as before; questions pressed upon him. Was this really Vilcapampa la Vieja? Or was it further on? He seemed deserted by the unseen ones who previously guided him upward, inspiring his consciousness, pushing him toward higher and higher conquests into the sky. This must be Vilcapampa!—but because he could never be sure, he simply named the city Machu Picchu. Why not give it the name of the stupendous peak upon which it rests?

Bingham returned to Peru in 1912 and again in 1913. After three expeditions (1911, 1912, 1913), he did not return to Peru until 1948—33 years after his last expedition. The Peruvian government asked him to cut the blue ribbon on a bridge over the Urubamba below Machu Picchu. The winding road—named the Hiram Bingham Road—which had been built up the side of Machu Picchu, had been completed. He returned to see it opened for travelers to reach the famous peak. He died in Washington on June 6, 1956.

The Hiram Bingham Road
At Puente Ruinas, travelers to Machu Picchu will take the
bus up Hiram Bingham Way, constructed in 1948 and
dedicated to the discoverer of Machu Picchu. This road
covers 6 miles and winds around 14 curves. Before
construction of the road, tourists climbed to the ruins by
foot on a path which still exists.

Chapter Eleven

The Intihuatana -- the Altar of Initiation

The heart of every mystic yearns to stand in the midst of this mysterious city and absorb its huaca. It has been called "the high holy place of the empire, a sentinel at the border of the four worlds, between heaven and earth." Only gods and god people could possibly have created such massive splendid walls, niches, lintels, portadas, andenes, stairways, buildings and mausoleums. And only such gods could have raised the stone of Intihuatana at its very summit.

The Indians were so protective of Machu Picchu, the City of Gold, that there are actually very few legends about its founding. To understand why the city of Machu Picchu is situated exactly where it is on the summit of Machu Picchu mountain one must not only be familiar with mundane astronomy but sacred astronomy. Only one familiar with both the mundane and the sacred in the heavens will ever be able to clearly understand why this mysterious city is situated exactly where it is in the midst of these spectacular peaks. Not only the apus, but all the celestial guardians of the heavens pour out their measure of divinity upon this holy site.

169

Even after its discovery by Hiram Bingham in 1911, Machu Picchu was still inaccessible to casual tourists for a long time. Where once it was a hard two or three days journey climbing the Inca Trail from Cuzco on muleback or on foot, it has now become accessible by train and motor. To accommodate some probably 30,000 tourists a year who come to view this magnificent cosmic ecstasy, there is now a train climbing the dizzying height from Cuzco up to the peaks of Machu Picchu. There is also a steel bridge spanning the waters of Rio del Sol, the River of the Sun. For several years, there has been a perilous road that winds upward, called the Hiram Bingham Highway, which one can drive. And of course airplanes can fly in, but it's a rather hazardous journey by air, even now. Most of the travelers, by far, arrive on the little train that travels up once a day.

On the train ride, the eye scans what probably are the most awesome visions nature has ever accomplished on this Earth planet. There is the Urubamba River flowing just outside the window of the train along the way, and then as one climbs, one looks down from unbelievable heights watching the river become a little ribbon of white—far, far below.

Either on the Inca Trail or on the train puffing its slow way to Machu Picchu, you might occasionally remember the many bloody battles that took place along the way. In other countries we've visited, the guides have made a great effort to point out the sites where famous battles occurred. But it was not done on the train ride from Cuzco to Machu Picchu, and that's where some of the most gruesome battles of the planet have occurred. In their struggle with the conquistadors from Spain thousands and thousands of Indians were slaughtered. Many of the most hideous battles took place along the train route.

Almost straight above you, piercing the sky like upraised arms, are the two towering peaks of Machu Picchu (Old Peak) and Huayna Picchu (Young Peak)— called young because it is still growing. Each could have been the Tower of Babel so poignantly do they struggle toward heaven. In fact, Machu Picchu is known as "the place where heaven meets earth." The peaks are often shrouded in clouds, beautiful white drifting clouds which quickly change from thick curtains to misty wisps, covering the peaks completely or curling about them like angel arms lovingly embracing.

Along the way, one is brought abruptly back to reality when the train stops at a midway station, Pachar, where many Peruvians crowd around trying to sell their wares. Beautiful Peruvian sweaters, scarves, jackets, belts, necklaces, blouses, souvenirs, even food is thrust upon you—anything the Indians have discovered that the tourists will buy.

The train travels slowly, requiring several hours, enabling the passengers gradually to become acclimated to the rare altitude. If one arrives suddenly, as by air, the stewardess warns the passengers to move and walk very slowly as they depart the plane. And even then, stepping suddenly into that altitude, some have been known to faint immediately from lack of oxygen. That was why so few of our group reached the summit of Machu Picchu where we buried the crystals we brought with us and viewed the massive Intihuatana. Many began the climb with me but one by one they dropped panting on the ascending steps or slopes. Only thirteen of us reached the stupendous summit—and only seven of us lingered to bury the crystal and the prayer petitions. I didn't even feel the lack of oxygen! I seemed to be upheld by some indescribable force—which has happened during every one of my innumerable journeys to mystical sites around the world.

Entering Machu Picchu

Before reaching the city the train arrives at its destination—the Puente Ruinas station. The travelers depart it to board a bus to complete the journey—which ends in front of the one small hotel on the glorious peak—Hotel Machu Picchu. There your group of travelers is met by the guide who will escort you about the city and babble off his or her memorized script as your group passes from one building to the next. Few guides are intuitive enough to have probed the true mystery of their daily task. Although Machu Picchu is actually 3,000 feet lower than Cuzco, it seems higher because of the stupendous huaca that radiates from the mountain—although it is likely the awe-inspiring panoramas that leave one with the feeling of breathless wonder.

The city perches on a pedestal of the old peak of Machu Picchu. Bottomless precipices surround it on every side except the one route followed by the little red train, the new highway and the partially hidden *Nan Cuna*—the old 625 mile road built long ago by the

Incas many years before Pizarro came. Only God could have planned it so—such a perfect pedestal with only one entrance.

Via that three and one half hour train ride you've entered both a new and an ancient world, a view so incredible you wonder if it's the altitude or the nearness of God that takes your breath away. There, 8,875 feet up into the high Andes, you've found the famous Lost City of the Incas. The magnificent ruins, the terraced gardens speak mutely of an ancient civilization that disappeared from our Earth centuries ago.

You remember that the last Inca was vanquished over 400 years ago and that the city lay shrouded in clouds and mystery since that faraway time. Viewing the ruined temples and palaces you remember that many of those consecrated to the sun god were once crowned with pure gold. And those consecrated to the moon with silver. The sight of that stupendous view is burned into your memory and your heart for all eternity. And you realize that after scaling these terraces and temples, you'll never be the same.

So many questions! Who were the gods and goddesses who built this magical paradise? And why? What was its purpose, perched here like a spread-out eagle's nest? What was its link to Tiahuanaco? You remember the Gate of the Sun there—the sun god carved on its massive lintel, holding a strange staff in each hand. And all those winged astronauts surrounding this cosmic traveler. Did they build Machu Picchu too? Was it a sister city? To where did they all vanish? And why?

Standing at the entrance and viewing the panorama without equal on this plane, the emanations, the rising vibrations, the swirling currents of energy are easily perceived before one even steps on the grounds of the sacred city, even if one is not supersensitive to them. The lifeforce even in this "dead" city is enhanced. One truly expects to see the welcoming outstretched hand of a great god emerging from around the bend of a monolithic altar.

Before venturing into the city it seems only natural to pause to say a prayer in the quiet recesses of the heart—a prayer that even a small portion of the magical essence will enter your soul, because, like an etheric baptism, the burst of God's glory that created this incredible other-world creation must still linger. The prayer is that some small portion may be absorbed—through the soles of the feet, through the heart, through the hands, through the intuitive qualities of the soul—that will leave a part of you forever among the wonders of this haunted height, and that will remain an innate part of you when you depart.

Standing at the only gateway, the Huaca Puncu—the *Gate of Honor*—at the end of the *Nan Cuna,* surveying the sleeping city, there is so much to see you wonder which direction to turn. But your eyes are drawn to the highest point. Poised on the summit of a man-made step pyramid sits the empty Intihuatana and the small deserted chapel nearby silhouetted against the sky, like watchtowers guarding the ghosts of the Sky People, the Builders of this sprawled magnificence.

The Gate of Honor
This was the access to Machu Picchu from Cuzco. The
doorway has a great lintel of stone and the stones of the
walls had to be carefully fitted to perfection.

The Chapel on the Summit
The stone chapel on the summit of Machu Picchu extending
so high into the clouds one despairs of ever reaching it.

Alarmed at the height of the climb toward the Intihuatana you despair of ever reaching it. Billows of white clouds drift around the peak as it sits silently brooding—and beckoning.

Then the eyes travel down to the upper city and the open plazas. Throughout the city are the tiered andenes upon which the stupendous hanging gardens once cascaded downward. They graced the city from the summit to the lower city and even tumbled over the canyon walls, interrupted by a seemingly endless waterfall which plunged into the wilderness below.

It is impossible to tread the andenes of Machu Picchu without absorbing the lifeforce exuded by the "Old Peak." Researchers have discovered Machu Picchu to be a veritable storehouse of negative ions which, added to the mysterious energy exuding from every megalithic stone, gives one a constant sense of vital force and exhilaration.

Breaking the trance of the summit which has engulfed you, your eyes cannot help but drop again to view the canyons and the lush jungles descending far below on the slopes of Machu Picchu mountain. The River of the Sun winds its way like a giant serpent around the base of the majestic peaks, the roar of its waters distant and muffled.

Entering the city, we retraced the footsteps of Hiram Bingham, the modern discoverer of Machu Picchu. I remembered that last day of Bingham's journey, as he climbed the torturous terrain seeking what the natives had called "the Lost City of Gold."

And the small Indian boy who had emerged from the misty fog and came toward him smiling. I remembered the smiling boy stepped off the summit into thick clouds and totally disappeared.

Yachay Huasi or the Central Group

Following in the noble footsteps of the long dead Incas, we passed through the Huaca Puncu, the sacred gateway, to the phenomenal Torreon of the Sun—the *Sumtur Huasi*—extending out over an enormous boulder. We passed through a long corridor of incredible rectangular buildings, most of which were two-storied—all of which boasted interior patios leading towards bedrooms, classrooms or workshops. The walls of the buildings were adorned with magnificent trapezoidal niches and portadas that seemed to be for security. This section seems to have been reserved for prominent personages.

Leaving the gateway, the path leads down into the city past the *tombs of the rock*—so called because Bingham exhumed mummies of the Virgins of the Sun from this royal mausoleum. Near these virgins' tombs stands a votive rock with carved steps that lead to its top. Archaeologists believe the dead were laid upon this rock altar as we now lay our important personages in state so that a final supreme homage may be offered. It seems strange that one must pass through these funerary facilities before entering the city proper. Is it because the Builders insisted you pause to pay homage to those who built the city, to offer a reverential acknowledgment to their wisdom, their courage, and, indeed, their technology? There can be little doubt that their holy spirits hovered among us. Their voices whispered just beyond the range of hearing.

Surveying this suspended jewel at the summit of this incredible peak, you stand stunned, surveying the stones of the monoliths which weigh several tons. They are quarried to absolute perfection. Who could have accomplished this unearthly feat? It is far beyond any accomplishment of any Earthean even today. These stone monoliths are certain proof of the presence of mysterious godpeople, who conceived Peru's age-old masterpiece. The city is mute proof of their presence and their power. The only way the city could have been built is with the wondrous lasers and advanced tools of the mysterious Builders. Certainly the presence of this magnificent handiwork proves the existence of the ingenious Builders of palaces, fortresses and sanctuaries in an architectural style unknown elsewhere in the world.

Hiram Bingham writes: "Machu Picchu lies like a petrified paradise, speaking mutely of a vanished glory. Smooth as an angel's skin, the stones of the monoliths—weighing several tons and quarried to perfection by who knows what titans capable of overcoming an inhuman terrain—are the only marks left by the mysterious godpeople who conceived Peru's imperishable, age-old masterpiece—proof of their superhuman power.

"One doesn't even now see the phantom city until the dizzy heights are reached. Then, around a bend in the path, there suddenly looms, like a mirage or a vision summoned by a magic wand, an entire city, so far from 'dead' it seems that any moment one may catch the flash of light flaming from the 'golden disk of the sun' sitting in its niche in the Torreon. And one even waits breathless for the god-beings to emerge from the colossal walls to greet you—the incomparable Builders who defied the laws of gravity and equilibrium to raise this incredible Eighth Wonder of the World. And even now, the mute stones defy our science to comprehend what magical feats the Builders accomplished to execute this megalithic marvel."

Again, what was its name when the god-beings lived here? Who were they? Where did they come from? Why did they come? Why did they build this forbidden city? Where did they go? Why did they go?

The architecture certainly is not Incan. The Incas never could have built it, any more than the ancient Egyptians could have built the Great Pyramid. After the sudden departure of its Builders, Machu Picchu lay deserted until the Incas used it to hide away their Virgins of the Sun—their nuns—when the Spaniards arrived. And it lay deserted again with the death of the last Inca.

The terraces or andenes are the basic structures on which the city was built. On these andenes were the agriculture of the city and the basis for housing structures. Machu Picchu could not have housed more than a 1000 to 1200 persons. And it had no recourse to industry of any kind. It was without a doubt built as a religious center or a retreat for very special people. Its origin is unknown. Being pre-Incan, it is many thousands of years older than most of the chronologers indicate. The structures are constructed by those who had the wisdom of the gods—a wisdom, even now, beyond Eartheans.

The Hanging Gardens of Machu Picchu

The renowned Hanging Garden of Semiramis in Babylon was recognized among the Seven Wonders of the World, but it could not have surpassed the wonder of these hanging gardens of Machu Picchu. Long vanished, their remnants still remain. The city from the summit to the abyss was ablaze with colored blooms, among which peeped the most exquisite of orchids—still found in the nearby rain forests.

Equally incredible were the andenes upon which the plants were planted and from which they hung. The creation of the andenes was a superhuman work in itself and was assuredly carried out by beings from another world. Most andenes were about twenty yards long, seven or eight yards wide, and about a third as high—but some were over 100 yards long. The Indians of primitive Peru could never have met so great a challenge. The andenes throughout Peru are works of wonder, but the symmetrical perfection of the andenes in the city of Machu Picchu is awesome.

Sumtur Huasi or the Torreon of the Sun

Still marveling, we arrived at the horseshoe-shaped tower built of immense uncapped boulders, the Torreon of the Sun. Similar to the famous solar temple in the Coricancha at Sacsahuaman, this tower is absolutely flawless and remains today one of the most

The Torreon
Bingham considered this building to be the architectural
wonder of all South America.

beautiful examples of stone masonry ever found in
either North or South America. The stones in the walls
appear to have grown together; there's not the slightest gap in them, and they are welded together without
mortar.

The Torreon is considered the masterpiece of the
Lost City. The entire rounded building crowns a
magical rock which serves as its pedestal. This impos-
ing boulder, which could have been an insurmountable impediment to less gifted architects, was used to
enhance the beauty of the entire structure. Harmoniz-
ing with the gargantuan stone, the architects of
Machu Picchu constructed the Torreon above it. Thus
using it was not an obstruction, but a means of
glorification.

After constructing the half circle Torreon there followed slow, patient rubbing with wet sand to polish its stones until, even today, they gleam with a sacred light. The Torreon is structured with mammoth monoliths at its base, the stones decreasing in size, course by course, as they reach toward the top. There they are rounded to perfection with no roof planned. The Builders expected this Torreon would be standing into the future, so to prevent possible breaks in the curved horseshoe walls, they alternated polyhedrons with rectangular stones to form a series of keys.

Along the Torreon's curvilinear wall the Builders carved interior niches, surmounted by great stone pegs. The greatest riddle is the three trapezoidal windows which look out over the upper city. It is my strong belief that these windows were used to balance the acoustical system of the golden Punchao. Golden symbols of the sun were mounted in them. The central window could have held the Punchao, a communication center with amplifiers in the two neighboring windows

Perhaps the Inca himself often communicated through the Punchao, speaking to the inhabitants of the city from his home in the upper city, but it is my belief the central window held a Punchao with an Ark of the Covenant through which the Sky Guardians spoke from their spaceships and directed the people of the holy city—perhaps even Viracocha himself or Lord Maru.

The Torreon was probably also used for governmental operations as *Sumtur Huasi* means house of government. The cave under the Torreon was one of the most venerated places in the city. Gracing the wall were tiered benches making it appear that this was a small stadium of some kind. One could either sit on these steps cut into the wall and meditate, or they could view sacred rites that were taking place in the center. The niches held some of the sacred mummies of departed Incas.

Standing in its midst, one feels the presence of the Great Ones, whose mummies once graced it. There is a niche also which once held a golden idol through

One of the Three Windows of the Torreon
The middle window could have housed the Punchao, with amplifiers in the other two windows (which are on either side of the horseshoe-shaped Torreon). The Punchao could have contained a communication system through which the beings in their overshadowing spaceships—the actual Builders of the city—guided the inhabitants in their initiation rituals and other religious festivals.

which the voices of the departed spoke to the living initiates. It was their oracle. The living initiates drank a special herbal concoction of coca leaves and vilca juice before beginning their seances. A tunnel entrance may someday be found hidden beneath this cave—perhaps an endless tunnel. One of its branches possibly leads through the mountain of Huayna Picchu, the neighboring peak.

Tunnels beneath the city may lead up a steep curved stairway to a precipice near the summit of Huayna Picchu. Seated there on that ledge several of the Great Ones—and one very special hierophant— could look down upon the city of Machu Picchu, especially during the initiatory rites conducted at the Intihuatana. Viewing these ceremonies, the great Ptah, seated on the precipice of Huayna Picchu, could speak to, could even perform the initiation rites himself, as his voice spoke through the golden symbol of the sun—an Ark of the Covenant—tied to the upstanding prism on the enormous stone of the Intihuatana.

A noted Peruvian researcher states that "at least one third of Machu Picchu is still hidden in the form of intricate underground passages." In 1970 a journalist and an archeologist studied the city and unearthed "five doorways leading to the underground passages of the city." At least one doorway is next to the great stairway that descends to the bottom of the lower city. "It has a clearly visible lintel and a solidly constructed stone door...in accordance with the order to block all the chinkanas (tunnels) when the city was abandoned." Almost all of these passages are furnished with altars, benches, platforms and niches.

There is a carving of a condor on a triangular slab on the floor which faces the rising sun. The condor was considered to be the "Messenger of the sun" in Inca mythology. Mystics believe its stone beak points to an endless tunnel, probably part of the system that leads to the throne at the top of Huayna Picchu.

Huayna Picchu

The dark green peak of Huayna Picchu defies the sky and the gods—it must be the top of the world. It's like looking down from a window in paradise. It towers over the city of Machu Picchu like an overshadowing guardian—a celestial oversoul.

Dr. Jose Manuel Estrada, a Venezuelan scholar, stated: "Since the tellurico-magnetic center of the earth has shifted thirty degrees to the south, it is now located in the heart of the Inca ruins of Machu Picchu."

Was Huayna Picchu the *axis mundi* (world axis) of the Incas—the supreme cosmic mountain from which there streamed torrents of inexhaustible energy? It cannot be denied that the exhilarating panoramas from the peak—of both sunrise and sunset—place Huayna Picchu in a singular position in South American cosmology.

Huayna Picchu was once solely reached by climbing the perilous Inca Trail and 600 stone steps cut precipitously into the side of the peak. The Inca Trail is replete with natural and God-made wonders. One such site is the Gateway to the Sun, *Inti Puncu,* which leads one to the pass overlooking Machu Picchu. Only the eagle when she flies or the gods in their flying ships could have chosen such a view. Ascending further up the Trail toward the peak of Huayna Picchu, you enter an incredible rain forest which embraces the ancient village of *Wini Wayna* ("forever young") named for a flower which grows there among the indescribable orchids. Such orchids are usually only found in rain forests.

The village was once a beautiful botanical vision of hanging gardens interspersed with cascades of flowing fountains beginning at the sun temple at the top and descending downward into the shadows of Urubamba Canyon. The buildings around the sun temple beckon the climber to pause in the opened windows to absorb the exquisite beauty of the lush jungle. Its green tentacles, peaks and canyons graduate downward into the steep abyss of the Vilcapampa cordillera on either side, interrupted by foaming waterfalls plunging thousands of feet to the turbulent Urubamba below.

Marquis de Wavrin, the first European to climb the Trail, called his path up Huayna Picchu a "stairway to death." There was barely room for both feet, and sometimes only room for one foot set down at an angle—as were the stairs ascending the pyramids in the Yucatan. Near the summit of Huayna Picchu the Trail led to a massive ledge extending out over the gaping canyon below. At the back of the ledge and opening into the mountain was a huge cave which formed, with the ledge, one enormous room. At the back of the cave opened a tunnel. The Marquis entered the tunnel around 1930 but could not proceed into it because of lack of air. Near the edge of the ledge he found several beautiful carved stone thrones, arranged so that those sitting in them had a perfect view looking down upon the summit of Machu Picchu and the initiation stone, the Intihuatana.

Sitting there, de Wavrin was delighted in his view of Machu Picchu. He noted three archeological sites among the ruins on a steep sided bluff that hadn't been investigated by researchers because their location was only observable from above. And he saw the remnants of the Nan Cuna, the Inca Road, trailing far off into the distance. He called Machu Picchu the cosmic mountain.

Seated there like a spacegod on his throne in heaven, one can gaze out upon what is probably the most panoramic and breathtaking view found on this planet—stretching out many miles and down the

Huayna Picchu towers over the city of Machu Picchu.

entire slope of the peak. Seated on this throne of the sun—the massive stone throne on the ledge perched at over 9,000 feet—one has a view of the entire Sacred Valley as far as Ollantaytambo.

When the sun appears at a certain angle, a most spectacular phenomenon occurs. Suddenly the shadow of whoever is seated on the main throne on the ledge—the Marquis in this case—is cast on an overhanging cloud and haloed by all the colors of the rainbow—an intense blue at the edge, gradually turning to an orange at the center. There the aura floats, the image responding to the floating cloud drifts. It hangs there like a holographic god suspended in space. The person seated on the throne can speak and the holographic image will echo that message.

From this vantage, the god on the throne could easily view the summit of Machu Picchu and could speak through a communication system to those gathered for initiation around the Intihuatana. Because such a colorful rainbow array also appeared around the gold idol tied to the peak on the Intihuatana stone, it was called a Prism, reflecting all the colors of the rainbow. It was through an Ark tied to the Prism that the voice of the hierophant, seated on the ledge of Huayna Picchu, could be heard.

When an initiate lay on the Intihuatana stone undergoing initiation, the mighty Ptah, the initiator, could sit on the throne on the ledge of Huayna Picchu, far above the scene, and observe the form of the new initiate entering a state of trance during which he or she experienced an out-of-body experience.

While the new initiate was out of body, the Ptah raised his or her spirit form to the peak of Huayna Picchu and entered the sacred tunnel—which led to many secrets deep inside the earth. One was a Hall of Records containing secret teachings unavailable to any on earth save the initiates of Machu Picchu. One was the huge Cave of Initiation, where the actual out-of-body initiation Ceremony occurred.

Legend says that when Old Peak (Machu Picchu) and Young Peak (Huayna Picchu) were cut off from contact with the world, they were connected only by means of the chinkana tunnels. Archeologists refused to believe this until some university students discovered an entrance to a deep labyrinth near a sacred boulder at the foot of Huayna Picchu. They managed to penetrate about twenty five feet into the tunnel before the ruins of previous cave-ins completely blocked the passage. They noted, however, that to that point the walls were lined with finely carved stone.

But one of the tunnels connects the ledge of Huayna Picchu to the heart of Machu Picchu, making the ledge of Huayna Picchu easily accessible without having to scale the dangerous slopes of the Inca Trail to reach the ledge and cave of Huayna Picchu. Also to be seen from the thrones on the ledge are other distant cities lost in the sacred valley, half covered by vegetation, totally inaccessible from the outside. Obviously, then, tunnels lead to these secret sites—an entire labyrinth of tunnels.

All around the Marquis, on top of Huayna Picchu, lay the ruins of another splendid city, overshadowing

We start the climb toward
the summit of the city.

Many of the group drop
to the stone steps unable
to complete the climb be-
cause of lack of oxygen.

On the trail far ahead a lone musician plays a lonely wail on a flute, welcoming us to the summit. The clouds swirl about us and lie like a billowing white blanket blocking the view below us.

I have brought with me a huge crystal and a package of prayer petitions to be buried at the summit.

all the others. It has not, however, withstood the elements as has Machu Picchu. But the first European explorer, the Marquis, could not imagine who could have possibly constructed such a site since it was accessible only by climbing the treacherous Inca Trail or through tunnels from Machu Picchu. How raise these megalithic stones? Sonic Levitation?

The Climb to the Intihuatana

The stairway to the Intihuatana was described by Hiram Bingham as being the most carefully constructed stairway in Machu Picchu.The steps were intersected by three flattened landings and the 14 tiers of this artificial pyramid which reached 75 feet into the sky. From the crown of the hill, the view plummets 1,500 feet over vertiginous andenes to the canyon below on one side and to a panoramic view of the city on the other.

There waited before me the summit. Without hesitation—as if drawn by an unseen force—I started climbing the stairway cut into the rocks—unnumbered steps, leading upward toward the sky. The stairway leading to the summit was itself incredible. Bordered on each side by a low stone wall, it required extremely careful construction. In some places it is often only wide enough for one, to allow for a slow procession. How I could have made the climb is unbelievable since I have a terror of heights. I waited for the terror to engulf me. It never did. Like Bingham, I heard the voices of godbeings, "Something waiting for you. Go!"

There at the very summit lies the massive mysterious Intihuatana Stone—carved of solid granite.

The guide drones out his memorized speech of how the ancient priests tied the sun to this stone each year. But I knew the stone to be an altar upon which initiates lay to experience initiation. An Ark of the Covenant communication center and an initiate undergoing an initiation were actually tied to the stone, the Prism.

From the summit, one views not only the entire sacred city but the entire sacred valley and the surrounding peaks. There are 75 steps leading toward the dizzying heights. Even after the steps end, one still climbs a path upward and upward toward the summit. There one sees four small chapels housed under one roof.

Ascending still further, one suddenly beholds the sacred center of this entire city. At the very center of this summit there rests a gigantic stone, one massive boulder weighing untold tons. This stone is the renowned Intihuatana. Only godmen could have raised it to such stupendous heights and placed it in so strategic a position. And then, using an instrument as yet unknown on Earth, carved the stone both horizontally and vertically, causing a peak called the Prism to rise at one end of it. The Prism is approximately three feet high.

Through the decades, archaeologists have speculated as to the purpose of this spectacular stone with its Prism. One senses an aura of cosmic eternity here by the magnificently carved symbol of Inti, the sun god. The Intihuatana seemed to have recorded the movements of the sun, moon and stars for the brilliant astrologers and philosophers of the Andes. "Inti Huatana" has been translated as "the place where Inti (the sun) celebrates." The sanctity of the site still reaches out to touch the soul of the seeker after all these centuries—especially one who may have experienced initiation on the sacred summit, lying on the Intihuatana.

One purpose of the massive stone, say the researchers, was to interpret and record the movement of the sun and stars—an astronomical observatory. That adds to the wonder of the wisdom of those who planned its placement. It had to be exactly situated.

Also this sacred stone sits on the very summit of a man-made pyramid, whose very structure causes a concentration of earth energies to rise to meet the downpouring rays of the sun. This "point" is one of the most potent energy centers on earth, equal to that created by Egypt's Great Pyramid. This summit is called the Sacred Cemetery or Acropolis. I can't imagine why—unless the body of the first great Inca, Manco Capac, may be buried there beneath the Intihuatana.

Some say the Intihuatana was a sacrificial stone, that victims were tied to the Prism. This is *not* correct. The Builders of such an incredible monument would never have built such an eternal structure simply for the purpose of blood sacrifice. That activity could have been practiced elsewhere and anywhere.

Some say—and the guides echo this unbelievable idea—that the high priest made a ritual of "tying the sun" to the Prism each year at the winter solstice, using a golden chain, to assure the sun's return to our hemisphere. Builders wise enough to place a massive universal calendar in so strategic a place—and at the summit of so wondrous a city—would certainly know the sun would return in its cosmic timing. This ceremony performed each year was actually a ceremony of initiation called the *Inti Raymi*.

The initiates well knew that the golden chain which was tied around the vertical standing rock—the Prism —acted as a lightning rod to attract and anchor electrical and solar power into the Intihuatana. The golden chain tied the Ark to the Prism. The summit on which the enormous stone block rested was in itself a charged area of the stupendous peak. The chain tied around the Prism released strong electrical impulses not only into the rock but into the entire peak on which the rock rested. The type of electrical and solar energy the initiates received from the sun rays was a type of energy not yet comprehended by earth's scientists.

Those who led the initiation celebration knew the stone was constructed to be a sacred altar. A solid gold Punchao, in the form of a seated god holding an Ark of the Covenant, was tied to the Prism. It was this sun god rather than the sun which was tied to the Prism. Through the oracle of the Punchao, the great god Inti, the sun god—perhaps Viracocha himself— spoke to the Willac Umu (high priest), to the candidate being initiated and to the priests celebrating the Inti Raymi. So the Punchao's Ark was, in this instance, a receiving station, a communication center, through which messages were received from space gods aloft in their orbiting spacecraft.

The idea of the priests tying the sun to a rock so that it would reenter the Southern Hemisphere and bring the lifeforce back to the planet was "religion" offered to the primitives and the peasants.

Not only did the Ptah speak from the ledge on Huayna Picchu, prophesying and guiding the Willac

Umu, but the souls of departed initiates and Incas spoke through the golden Punchao. The researchers have never discovered the *real* secret of the Intihuatana—that it was a temple altar of initiation, just as the King's Chamber and the granite sarcophagus in the Great Pyramid was the most sacred site for initiation in ancient Egypt. And just as the granite altar in the highest tower at Palenque in the Yucatan was the site of initiation.

The initiate lay on the massive stone slab, just in front of the gold idol tied to the Prism, surrounded by the Willac Umu and the Melchizedeks of Peru. As the candidate for initiation and the Ptahs in Egypt drank the sacred soma juice, so those at Machu Picchu drank the juices of the sacred vilca plant and coca leaf. It was this vilca juice which helped the initiates and the Willac Umu to enter a trance, leave their bodies and travel through celestial heights to experience initiation for and with the candidate.

Vilca means "sacred" and this plant still abounds on the tropical slopes of Machu Picchu. The roots, the juice, the bark and the seeds, often mixed with coca leaves and chicha, were used by the hierophants to enter a state of hallucination or a state of hypnotic sleep. In this state, the priests and initiates experienced supernatural visions and came in touch with the spirits of departed Incas and priests. In the old days, and perhaps even now, holy persons entering altered states of ecstasy, prophesy to people. They discern the cause of illnesses and they cast out spirits obsessing others. The plant was used extensively by the Amautas, the famous great saints of Peru—the

outstanding psychics of the entire empire. That's why
the City of Gold—Machu Picchu—*was* called "Vilcapampa"—the "place where the Vilca grows."

Again, only thirteen of us reached the breathtaking
heights of the summit where the small stone chapel
and the Intihuatana stood. And only seven of us
remained to gather at the tiny chapel to bury the
crystals in a wall of the chapel and to link all the other
sacred centers of Earth to this energy center. But I
realized the stone's supreme importance. I knew
immediately the Intihuatana was a ceremonial altar
for initiation, as was the massive stone altar at
Palenque in the Yucatan. I realized, too, the stone was
granite, which means it was an enormous crystal as is
the granite sarcophagus in Egypt's Great Pyramid and
the stone altar at Palenque. Actually the entire city of
Machu Picchu is constructed of massive granite stones
—which means it is truly a crystal city.

As I stood on the summit with the wisps of clouds
billowing about me, with my hand touching the Intihuatana, my consciousness opened to a vision of a
long ago event, perhaps intuitively perceived or perhaps a glimpse of a previous lifetime. In the vision, I
stood in a stone temple viewing another immense altar
in the center of a pavilion. On the altar rested a
tremendous naturally formed crystal. From its center
radiated a shining bright light. I knew instinctively
that the light had been burning for centuries and I
knew it would burn for centuries to come.

The light ebbed and rose, sometimes so brilliant I
raised my hand or lowered my head to shield my eyes,

Burying the crystal and prayer petitions in the
wall of the small chapel.

Suddenly I saw an enormous crystal with an eternal
flame in its heart blazing upon the top of the Prism.

sometimes ebbing to a soft candle glow, but always radiating. Instinctively I knew the temple in which I stood was a sun temple. The crystal with its dazzling brilliance symbolized the sun. The light of the crystal, like the sun, would never be extinguished. There seemed to be liquid gold in its center upon which some unknown light shone so directly the gold reflected its brilliance. Who can ever know the secret of these eternal lamps embedded in the heart of a crystal? Could it too have been a crystal of eternal flames?

Where was I and that marvelous stone temple? Perhaps it could only have been in long-ago Atlantis. A mammoth crystal with an eternal light burning in its heart was in no current temple on Earth. It must have been Atlantis—or in one of my out-of-body experiences traveling on the astral plane in a temple of initiation. Or on the planet Sirius where I once went for an initiation.* Had I read about it somewhere or did my unseen Teacher impress it into my mind? There, in Machu Picchu, with my hand on the Intihuatana, I clearly "saw" a temple built of enormous stones.

The walls of the temple were constructed of them. Some of the stones were immense. They were interspersed with smaller stones with an inner glowing light—like huge crystal stones—so that the entire interior of the temple was eternally lighted and shone like sunlight at noon. The mammoth stones—both ordinary and crystal—dovetailed together perfectly. How long ago did I actually stand in that lighted temple?

*See my book *Initiation in the Great Pyramid* available at your favorite bookstore or from Astara, 800 W. Arrow Hwy., Upland, CA 91786.

Suddenly the temple surrounding me vanished and I stood again touching the Intihuatana on Machu Picchu. I saw a lighted crystal flaming on top of the Prism. I saw tied to that perpendicular Prism another strange marker. The Incas called it *Iuracrunu*—the Oracle—of Machu Picchu. It possessed a communication center emitting both voice and pictures, much as a television screen does in our homes today.

I thought of our NASA center in Houston, Texas communicating with our astronauts as they walked on the moon—except that with the initiations on the Intihuatana stone at Machu Picchu it was the other way around—the Ptahs, hierophants, and Melchizedeks had their space station in their spaceship aloft, communicating through this peculiar Iuracrunu "Ark of the Covenant" tied to the Prism of Intihuatana. And the Ptahs sitting atop Huayna Picchu could use the Iuracrunu to speak to the Peruvian priests and initiates during the initiation ceremony conducted around the Intihuatana. It was the voice of the Ptah speaking through the communication center

I saw the golden Punchao tied to the Prism with a gold cord which acted as a rod of power, drawing a mysterious solar energy into the stone. It was through the Punchao that the hierophant, seated on a ledge near the summit of Huayna Picchu, spoke to and actually conducted the ceremony of initiation here on the summit of Machu Picchu.

which gave the secret words which opened the tunnels below in the city of Machu Picchu.

Could Viracocha have come from Atlantis bringing this white shining crystal with him to Machu Picchu? Did comparable altars in the city of Tiahuanaco once hold a similar eternally lighted shining stone? Did the Prism crystal on the Intihuatana once pull down the rays of the sun like a magnifying glass—like a lightning rod attracts electricity? Could the stone then have endowed the stupendous Intihuatana with the living energy of the sun?

Is that how the priests "tied the sun" annually to Intihuatana for the initiates to lie upon and enter the state of blessedness? Did an unseen perpetual lamp burn there in the form of a magnificent, glistening crystal? Did the Sky People who built Machu Picchu bring these lighted crystals with them from their faraway planets as they brought the Arks of the Covenant? Did the mammoth crystal capstone that once graced the Great Pyramid burn with just such an eternal light? Whatever happened to the lighted stones when Atlantis fell? Did they plunge to the bottom of the ocean? Are they burning still? Will we ever learn how to light such a crystal again?

The entire vision faded. The rain was cold upon my face. The clouds were threatening as if to scold me for having penetrated a long-hidden secret. Why couldn't I also fathom the answer to so many of my questions?

Whether or not archaeologists will ever accept the fact that Machu Picchu was an initiation site is doubtful. Peruvian historian General F. de la Barra states:

"Of the seven acknowledged Wonders of the World —the hanging gardens of Babylon, the temple of Artemis at Ephesus, the statue of Zeus at Olympia, the Colossus at Rhodes, the Mausoleum at Halicarnassus, and the lighthouse at Alexandria—all have been destroyed by the elements or swallowed up by prehistory and legend. All that remains is the famous Great Pyramid of Egypt! Alongside it, Machu Picchu deserves the rank of Eighth Wonder of the World..."

After my vision of the lighted crystal atop the Prism of the Intihuatana in Machu Picchu, we secured a mammoth crystal to be used as a part of our own sacred initiation ceremony at our Mystery School in California. Once a year it is lighted within to project radiant rays upon the new initiates. During the year it acts as a focal point for our prayers projected throughout our planet. We pray for our overshadowing teachers to keep their own Eternal Flame burning in its heart.

Astara's beautiful crystal.

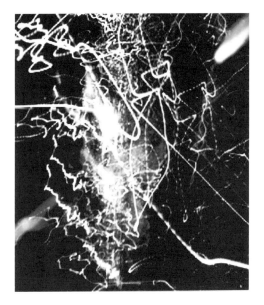

This picture was taken as I stepped away from the Intihuatana. These same flashes of light were in evidence as we buried the crystals in the wall of the chapel. Perhaps it reflects the tremendous emanations pouring into and through the Intihuatana. Perhaps it also captures some of the light rays pouring from the mammoth crystal and the smaller crystals we buried.

GLOSSARY

Acllas—Virgins of the Sun.

Amauta—teachers, wise men.

Apacita—pile of stones, usually to mark spot of great Huaca.

Apu—spirit of the mountain.

Aymara—people of Lake Titicaca area.

Ceque—ley line.

Chicha—fermented corn or quinoa drink.

Chinkanas—tunnels.

Cordillera—mountain range.

Coricancha—Temple of the Sun inside the fort of
   Sacsahuaman.

Huaca—magic/holiness/a place of great cosmic power.

Huacas—shrines.

Inti—the Sun/sun god.

Inti Raymi—winter solstice; initiation ceremony.

Mama Cuna—Mother superior of Virgins of the Sun.

Mama Quilla—the moon.

Nan Cuna—Inca road that ran from Ecuador to Chile.

Pacha Mama—Mother Earth.

Punchao—golden symbol of the sun and communicator
   usually kept in Coricancha.

Quechua—people and language from near Cuzco.

Quipu—series of knotted strings used for record keeping.

Quipu Camayoc—record keeper/rememberer.

Sacsahuaman—renowned fortress near Cuzco.

Salcantay—Sacred Mountain of Eternal Snows.

Tahuantinsuyo—the four corners of the world; the Inca Empire.

Viracocha—creator god.

Willac Umu—high priest.

BIBLIOGRAPHY

Berlitz, Charles. *Mysteries from Forgotten Worlds*
Double Day & Co., Garden City, NY

Bingham, Hiram. *Lost City of the Incas*
Atheneum paperback, New York, New York 1963

Valla, Jean-Claude. *The Civilization of the Incas*
Ferni Publishers, Geneva, 1978

Van Daniken, Erich. *Chariot of the Gods?*
G.P.Putman's Sons, New York, New York 1970

_____ .*Gods From Outer Space*
G.P.Putman's Sons, New York, New York 1970

_____ .*The Gold of the Gods*
G.P.Putman's Sons, New York, New York 1973

Waisbard, Simone. *The Mysteries of Machu Picchu*
Avon Books, New York, New York 1979

Wilkins, Harold T. *Mysteries of Ancient South America*
Citadel Press, New Jersey 1974

A MESSAGE FROM ASTARA

The publishers of this book have made it available to you in the belief that it will make a contribution to your life on its various important levels: physical, emotional, intellectual and spiritual.

Actually, we consider this volume to be an extension of the teachings contained in Astara's series of mystical studies known as *Astara's Book of Life*. The lessons comprising the *Book of Life* are distributed on a worldwide basis only to members of Astara. Astara was founded in 1951 as a nonprofit religious and educational organization including the following concepts:

1. A center of all religions oriented to mystical Christianity but accepting all religions as beneficial to humankind.

2. A School of the ancient Mysteries offering a compendium of the esoteric and mystical teachings of all ages.

3. A spiritual source embracing all philosophies coordinating many viewpoints of humankind and the interacting inner structures which unite us as one in the infinite.

4. An institute of metaphysical research and practice dedicated to physical, emotional, and spiritual healing and wholeness.

If these areas of activities appeal to you, you may wish to request information about Astara, its teachings, and other services. We have prepared a treatise entitled *Finding Your Place in the Golden Age.* You may have it without cost or obligation. Write:

ASTARA
P.O. Box 5003
Upland, CA 91785-5003

ALSO BY EARLYNE CHANEY

Initiation
in the
Great Pyramid

Join Earlyne Chaney through visions of another lifetime while in the sarcophagus of the Great Pyramid. There, in an altered state of consciousness, she encounters the hazards of initiation and the rigorous training to become a priestess of Melchizedek.

Visit again (for perhaps you have done so in the past) with wise teachers who tell how to work with your three selves, how to harmonize the Ba (conscious) and the Ka (subconscious) with the Aumakhua (superconscious).

Learn the astonishing story of how and when the Great Pyramid was built by the immortal Thoth. See through enlightened eyes the initiation ceremonies within its protective walls, passages, and chambers, especially the "Chamber of Transmutation." Receive the absorbing description of the Great Pyramid as a gigantic crystal with the now missing capstone of living light held in suspension above it.

Meet the remarkable Anaki, a people from "elsewhere," who married earth people and introduced "a stream of divinity" to Atlantis which later, in diminished form, was spread to other countries around the world. For your enlightenment and enjoyment, here is the story of a mystical journey. **$14.95**

Available at your bookstore or Astara

ALSO BY EARLYNE CHANEY

The Madonna
and the
Coming Light

Travel with Earlyne Chaney to ancient Ephesus, once majestic world center for sacred initiations and mystical philosophy. Share the spiritual quest to the Madonna's home there.

Join the author on her moving journey to the village of Medjugorje (in the former Yugoslavia) where six visionaries have been seeing and speaking with the Virgin since 1981. Read of the prophecies and promises.

Share the incredible disclosures of the Virgin to the apostles concerning reincarnation in the *Lost Book of Acts*—as the Madonna reveals the past lives of herself and her son Jesus and their last lives in Jerusalem—fascinating truths as she lay on her death bed.

In *Madonna and the Coming Light* Chaney tells of the coming changes as the world passes from the Piscean Age into the Aquarian Age and how each of us will be affected by the closing of the "Cosmic Door." She explains the phenomena of the "falling crosses," and reveals how it relates to the coming light of the Aquarian Age. **$15.95**

Available at your bookstore or Astara

ALSO FROM ASTARA

Ten Steps to Self Fulfillment

by Robert Chaney

Read it for fun because it's just plain interesting

Read it for profit because it helps improve the way you work, your relationships with others, and the attainment of your goals

Read it for self fulfillment because it helps bring your unused potentials to the surface of your life

Read it for more satisfaction with life because it gives you insight into the meaning of your own life and the fulfillment of your life mission

Read it now and save because this is the same material sold in lesson form for $35—now a soft cover book for only **$15.95.**

Available at your bookstore or Astara

Other Books Available From Astara

Secret Wisdom of the Great Initiates, E. Chaney. Share the wisdom of the great philosophers. Socrates, Plato, Apollonius, and Pythagoras. **$15.95**

Lost Secrets of the Mystery Schools, E. Chaney. Learn how the teachings of the Greek Mystery Schools relate to you in the present day. **$15.95**

Remembering: The Autobiography of a Mystic, E. Chaney. A story of suspense and enlightenment—true, dramatic, humorous. A true story of life after death. **$11.95**

Revelations of Things to Come, E. Chaney. The future through 2000 and further; ancient and modern space gods; Doomsday or Coming Light? **$13.95**

The Mystery of Death and Dying, E. Chaney. Learn of the potential for the Initiation of Liberation at the hour of death; of the seed atoms; of the Clear Light of salvation; of the "birth " of kundalini and how to assure immortality of the soul through the transition called death. **$10.95**

Secrets From Mt. Shasta, E. Chaney. A suspenseful spiritual out-of-body journey to the higher spheres to participate in an initiation. Complete with illustrations and photos. **$8.95**

The Eyes Have It, E. Chaney. Explore the relationship between the physical and spiritual eye, achieving the best possible eyesight and maintaining it through natural methods. **$9.95**

Forever Young, E. Chaney. Techniques for both men and women to maintain youthful beauty and vigor. Eliminate sagging muscles and aching joints with natural treatment methods. **$12.95**

The You Book, E. Chaney. Holistic methods and techniques for obtaining and maintaining physical health and vitality. **$16.95**

Kundalini and the Third Eye, E. Chaney/W. Messick. Mystical esoteric, psychic, and historical; ancient rituals; yogic and breathing techniques; 70 illustrations. **$12.95**

The Essenes and Their Ancient Mysteries, R. Chaney. Discover the Essenes' teachings about angelology, baptism, immortality, prophecy, healing, and more. **$5.95**

***Occult Hypnotism,* R. Chaney.** Uses of hypnotism for healing, astral projection, clairvoyance; ideas for personal experiments. **$4.95**

***The Inner Way,* R. Chaney.** Simple inner attunement meditations that will help in dealing with personal problems and focusing your entire being toward your life's goals. **$9.95**

***Think on New Levels,* R. Chaney.** Ways to approach work, personal relationships, and your own Self with new understanding. **$4.95**

***Transmutation: How the Alchemists Turned Lead Into Gold,* R. Chaney.** Ancient and modern alchemical ideas seen as philosophical concepts for self-unfoldment. **$4.95**

***Mysticism—The Journey Within,* R. Chaney.** A workable approach to mystical awareness and self-development. If you've ever had a mystical experience, this book is for you. **$13.95**

***Unfolding the Third Eye,* R. Chaney.** Steady seller since 1970; explains the third eye, its functions, and gives ways to tap its potential. **$4.95**

***Reincarnation—Cycle of Opportunity,* R. Chaney.** Answers questions about being a newborn again, wanting to return vs. having to, time between incarnations, how you incarnate, more **$4.95**

Current publications and prices available at:

**Astara, Inc.
800 W. Arrow Hwy.
P.O. Box 5003
Upland, CA 91785-5003**